The Big Picture
Table of Contents

CROSS-CULTURAL DISCUSSION ARTICLES 6
YOU USE CHOPSTICKS VERY WELL 7
WHAT IS ISHIN DENSHIN? 11
COFFEE AND DOUGHNUTS 14
NO IS NOT A FOUR LETTER WORD 19
AMBIGUITY, VAGUENESS AND THE UNKNOWN 22
LOOKING IN THE MIRROR 27
CROSS-CULTURAL VOCABULARY REVIEW 30

PEOPLE DISCUSSION ARTICLES 34
ANOTHER DAY IN THE RAT RACE 35
THE FOURTH TYPE 38
I WEAR MY HEART UPON MY SLEEVE 42
I'M SHY 46
BEING GREAT 50
CLOTHES MAKE THE MAN AND WOMAN 54
PEOPLE ARTICLES VOCABULARY REVIEW 58

HUMAN RESOURCES DISCUSSION ARTICLES 62
MY BOSS HAS NO CLOTHES 63
IT'S JUST BUSINESS, NOTHING PERSONAL 67
I'M SO TIRED, MY MIND IS ON THE BLINK 70
LIFO 74
HELP WANTED, BUT ONLY IF… 78
HUMAN RESOURCES VOCABULARY REVIEW 83

IT DISCUSSION ARTICLES 86
TWO SIDES OF THE COIN 87
GEEKS VS. SUITS 90
1984 MAY STILL BE COMING 94
NOISE FROM THE KNOWLEDGE 98
IT ARTICLES VOCABULARY REVIEW 102

The Big Picture
Table of Contents

SUCCESS DISCUSSION ARTICLES 106
- EQ • IQ (PART 1) 107
- WORK YOUR TAIL OFF 110
- TRUE GRIT (PART 3) 114
- LUCK OF THE DRAW (PART 4) 118
- LOOKS+HEIGHT=SUCCESS (PART 5) 122
- MEETING TRIUMPH AND DISASTER 126
- SUCCESS ARTICLES VOCABULARY REVIEW 130

MANAGEMENT DISCUSSION ARTICLES 134
- ORGANIC VS. NON-ORGANIC 135
- THE IMPORTANCE OF QUESTIONS 138
- A DELICATE BALANCE 142
- THE BUCK NO LONGER STOPS ANYWHERE 146
- MANAGEMENT ARTICLES VOCABULARY REVIEW 151

MARKETING DISCUSSION ARTICLES 154
- WALK A MILE IN MY SHOES 155
- WEAPONS OF MASS PERSUASION 160
- PARISIAN LOVE 162
- THE ETERNAL MARKETING BUZZWORD BRAND 166
- MARKETING ARTICLES VOCABULARY REVIEW 170

MISCELLANEOUS DISCUSSION ARTICLES 174
- THE DISEASE OF NOT LISTENING 175
- PLAY THE MAN ACROSS FROM YOU 178
- THE GOLDEN RULE 182
- EUREKA! 186
- PLAY BALL! 190
- MISCELLANEOUS ARTICLES VOCABULARY REVIEW 194

TEXTBOOK REVIEW 197

What is the Big Picture?

This textbook's purpose is for business English students to improve their vocabulary and discussion skills. Each unit integrates both vocabulary and discussion activities so students can improve their language skills and increase their confidence in speaking. In addition, the text has a small amount of grammar and a few role-plays. It is for intermediate level students and above.

Why is a larger vocabulary important? A larger vocabulary allows people to be better communicators. They can express themselves more clearly, and with more precision, which will make them more confident in their English abilities. A rich, well-developed vocabulary makes someone a better contributor to meetings, and a better thinker who can make connections between various topics. Moreover, expanding a vocabulary will allow him or her to better understand the world around them—to read between the lines, and quickly question what others have to say.

Before explaining why discussions skills are important, they first need to be defined. Discussion skills are listening, arguing, persuading, questioning and informing. All of these skills improve when someone has a larger vocabulary.

Discussion skills are important as business people need to employ them in meetings, conferences and interviews. In business, discussions are integral so a subject can be more deeply understood. They allow people to explore ideas and exchange information as well as expanding and clarifying knowledge. It also lets an issue be analyzed and its merits weighed. By improving discussion skills, a group can make a wiser decision or reach a conclusion with more speed.

How are students supposed to use this textbook? Each week their teacher will assign an article to read along with activities to do before the class. The students should do the activities and reading, so when class starts they have the necessary vocabulary to discuss the topic. The activities are designed for students to increase their vocabulary and use the words in the proper context. Students cannot contribute to the lesson unless they are well prepared.

In class, the teachers should review the answers and then the class should have a discussion. When the students have a discussion, they should understand that the discussion is not a race. Topics should be discussed thoroughly. Students should elicit their classmates' opinions, make sure the other students give reasons and ask follow up questions if necessary.

The subject matter for the articles is not based on the latest news or events, but is about ideas, research and issues that are being discussed in business schools, media and business. Some of the opinions put forth in the articles people may disagree with. Students and teachers should feel free to do so, but as users of this text make sure everyone's arguments are well structured and thought out.

This book was an accident as it started out as additional reading activities for a different textbook I was developing. After some time, I realized that I almost had enough material for a book. I have used these articles and their accompanying activities with my company classes at Rakuten, Mitsui Fudosan, Citibank, Novartis and PwC etc. I would like to thank all of those students for their time and effort and being my test subjects.

There is one class I would especially like to thank, my Saturday private group class known as Tokyo Nihonjins who have been my primary guinea pigs, Ryotaro Yanagawa, Takahiro Shirouzu, Masami Sakamaki, Akihiro Kondo, Ami Shinoda and Go Sato have been a pleasure to teach over the last five years.

While writing a book is a solo endeavor, it still is helpful to have people to help polish it. I would like to thank many people for helping me in the development of this textbook. First, I would like to express thanks to Everett Ofori, Andrew Gleboff and Andrew Wilson for their input and proofreading and Cal Bolick who redesigned the Lesson Notes page many years ago. I would also like to thank Chie Ando for the translation on the next page and Lapis Design for the front cover. I would especially like to thank Diana Camargo and Courtney Dobrzykowski for their help in proofreading, support and input. For any and all errors you may find, I apologize in advance for them if they cause any trouble. There is one person whom I can never show enough appreciation, Masami Kojima. She has done research, wrote the kanji for one of the chapters and given me enthusiastic support during my 3 years of writing this book.

© David Baird

What is the Big Picture?

概要

　本書は、ビジネス英語において必要なボキャブラリー、語彙力とディスカッションスキルを向上させるための要点をまとめたテキストであり、英語中級者から上級者向けとなっています。各章では、登場した英単語とディスカッションの際の使用例が記載されており、英語力の向上だけでなく、英語を話すことへの自信を深めることができます。リスニングには非対応ですが、文法についても簡単に触れています。

　ビジネスシーンにおいて英語を話す時、なぜ豊富な語彙力が重要となるのでしょう？豊富な語彙力があれば、自信を持って英語を話せるようになるだけでなく、自分の意見を効果的かつ明確に表現できるようになり、円滑なコミュニケーションを可能にします。また会議での様々なテーマに対し、洗練された説得力のある発言ができるでしょう。さらに語彙力を強化することで理解力も鍛えられ、行間を読むことも、また状況に応じた臨機応変な質問も出来るようになります。

　次にディスカッションスキルが何故重要となるのかを説明する前に、まずディスカッションの定義を正しく理解しましょう。聴く、議論する、説得する、質問する、情報交換する、がディスカッションの要素であり、豊富な語彙力、表現力を身につけることはこれら全てにおいて効果的です。

　ディスカッションスキルはビジネスシーン–顧客訪問、会議、採用面接などで必要不可欠です。このスキルを身につけることで、テーマに対する知識が広がり、論点を明確にすることができます。また、お互いの意見や情報を交換することで、メリットとデメリットを充分に分析し、建設的な議論が可能になります。ディスカッションスキルが向上すれば、より深くより良い結論を短時間で出すことができるでしょう。

　それではみなさんはどのようにこのテキストを使えばいいのでしょうか。毎週、講師がテキストを予習するよう指示します。みなさんは予習によって、授業で議論するために必要な語彙力を事前に身につけます。テキストは語彙力、表現力の向上を意図して作られています。しっかりと予習し積極的に授業に参加しましょう。

　授業では講師が簡単な要点をまとめた後に、みなさんでディスカッションを行います。ディスカッションは相手を打ち負かすことが目的ではありません。お互いに冷静な質疑応答をし、質問に対してしっかりとした説明が出来るようにしましょう。また議論を深めるために必要であれば、積極的に追加の質問をしましょう。

　ディスカッションテーマは最新のニュースや出来事ではなく、ビジネススクールやメディア、ビジネスシーンで実際に論じられている発想、研究、問題についてです。これらの多くは過去30年に多く取り上げられ議論されてきましたが、今後30年においても同様に議論されていくでしょう。

　挙げられたいくつかのポイントや意見には賛成できないものもあるかもしれません。もちろん全てに賛成できなくても構いませんが、自身の議論をより論理的で洗練されたものにしましょう。

All rights reserved; no part of this publication may be reproduced, stored in a retrieval system, or transmitted in any form or by any means electronic, mechanical, photocopying, recording or otherwise without the prior written permission of David Baird.

©David Baird 2015

Cross-Cultural Discussion Articles

You Use Chopsticks Very Well

Warm Up

Classroom Discussion Questions
1. How good are your table manners?
2. What are good small talk topics?
3. A colleague is meeting an overseas business associate for the first time and is quite nervous, as he has had very little contact with any foreigners. What advice would you give him or her?
4. What is your technique to make someone feel comfortable when meeting him or her?

Vocabulary Finding Activity

A. Find the words in the article that mean
1. refinement   _____
2. praise   _____
3. insinuated   _____
4. marvelous   _____
5. mostly   _____
6. say differently   _____
7. valued   _____
8. viewpoint   _____

B. Choose four of the words that you have found for the above vocabulary exercise and write four sentences below using each of those words in a sentence.
1. _____
2. _____
3. _____
4. _____

Polite Question Match

Match the phrase with a more polite question

1. When will you go back to your country?
2. Why did you come to the party?
3. Can you drink green tea?
4. What kind of food can you eat?
5. Does your country have four seasons?
6. Do you like Japanese food?
7. Why are you so; big, fat, tall?
8. What is your blood type?

a) Would you like some green tea?
b) Avoid making a negative comment or ask a question about people's appearance.
c) What's your favorite Japanese dish?
d) Do you think you will retire in Japan?
e) Have you ever heard about Japanese superstitions regarding blood type?
f) What brings you here tonight?
g) What kind of food do you prefer?
h) So how's the weather in your hometown?

Compliment Activity

If you were to meet someone for the first time, what are three typical compliments you could give him or her? Write them down below.

1. _____
2. _____
3. _____

Backhanded Compliment Activity

After completing the reading, give an example of a backhanded compliment. Create the context if needed.

_____
_____
_____

© David Baird

You Use Chopsticks Very Well

You are sitting down for dinner in a nice elegant Japanese restaurant with a business associate from the UK. He uses his chopsticks with grace and dexterity, so you compliment him on his skill, "You use chopsticks very well." Your business associate looks insulted and then curtly replies, "Thank you."

What went wrong? What did you say? You used correct English. You meant to compliment him, but his response made you feel like you said something wrong. The problem is a matter of context and implied meaning.

From personal experience, you have seen many Westerners not being able to use chopsticks well. As well, you think that many young Japanese are clumsy when using chopsticks, so you are puzzled by your visitor's reaction. However, your foreign guest may have interpreted the compliment as "You use chopsticks very well, (*for a foreigner but not as good as a Japanese person*)." He probably believes that this phrase is not something you would normally say to a Japanese coworker. Nor would he ever consider telling a Japanese person that they use a knife and fork very well.

He feels that you have given him a backhanded compliment which is an insult disguised as a compliment, usually used to show contempt. The structure of backhanded compliments is first some initial praise mixed in with some implied criticism. "That dress is fabulous as it makes you look slender," is an example of a backhanded compliment as the statement implies that the woman normally looks fat.

When learning your native tongue and growing up, you learn what is appropriate and inappropriate to say from experience, observations and instruction. You also learn to how to read ambiguous remarks or situations because you understand the manner, place, time, etc., of an utterance.

However living in your country will probably give you little opportunity to get experience speaking a foreign tongue outside a classroom. As you learn a foreign language at school, television programs or via the Internet, the primary focus is on using correct grammatical language; therefore, if your speech follows proper grammar rules when speaking your discourse is then correct. On the other hand predominantly focusing on correct sentence structure can cause an awkward social interaction.

So how do learn to give a compliment in a foreign language? Move to the country so you can practice with native speakers? Say nothing so that way you will never offend anyone? Get a better teacher? The best answer is neither silence nor moving to a foreign country to get real experience nor getting a new teacher. Silence is not appreciated in social situations as most Westerners find it uncomfortable and awkward. As for moving to a foreign country, it can speed up the learning process in many instances and offer more opportunity for interaction, but it is not practical as it takes considerable time and money.

Now, as for needing a new teacher, perhaps a better thing would be to utilize your teacher differently. Be more precise when asking your instructor for advice such as, "Is that phrase authentic? What would you (the teacher) say in this type of situation?" Nonetheless, do not rely on just one teacher as each teacher has a different cultural perspective and background. Additionally you can use movies and TV to see how compliments are given.

Still the best advice is to go ahead with your usual comments and questions, but pay more attention to people's reactions. If you get a negative reaction, then try to rephrase and clarify what you wanted to articulate. If a similar opportunity arises again then you will know from experience what to say.

© David Baird

You Use Chopsticks Very Well Activity Sheet

True and False Quiz
Based on the reading, circle whether the statements below are true or false.
1. Foreigners are always pleased to hear that they use chopsticks very well. — True/False
2. A backhanded compliment is the best kind of compliment to give. — True/False
3. When growing up, most people learn what is appropriate to say. — True/False
4. Westerners enjoy silence when meeting people. — True/False
5. Going abroad to learn a foreign language is effective and cheap. — True/False
6. If you find a good language teacher, always use him or her. — True/False
7. Genuine examples of English can be found on the Internet, in books and movies but not in magazines. — True/False
8. Knowing how to converse properly in a foreign language can help people communicate better in their language. — True/False

Vocabulary Matching Activity
A. Match the words from the article on the left with the synonyms on the right.

1) dexterity   a) uncoordinated
2) insulted   b) personal communication
3) curtly   c) unsuitable
4) context   d) situation
5) clumsy   e) evaluations
6) inappropriate   f) real
7) observations   g) express
8) social interaction   h) abruptly
9) authentic   i) offended
10) articulate   j) skillfulness

B. Now, choose five of the words from the above vocabulary exercise on the left side and write five sentences below using each of those words in a sentence.
a) _____
b) _____
c) _____
d) _____
e) _____

Classroom Discussion Questions
Write your discussion questions based on the article. Next, ask your classmates your questions and make sure they give reasons. Ask follow up questions if necessary.

a) _____
b) _____
c) _____
d) _____
e) _____

Additional Questions for Discussion
Discuss the questions below with your classmates. Give your reasons.

1. What would be a foolish thing to say when meeting someone for the first time?
2. Do you agree, "You use chopsticks well," is a strange compliment to make?
3. Have you ever asked a rude question or made an impolite comment when meeting someone? If yes, what was it?
4. What would be a rude question to ask in your native language?
5. When meeting a Japanese person, what do you normally talk about?
6. When meeting a foreigner, what do you normally talk about?
7. Have you ever asked a teacher a rude question?

You Use Chopsticks Very Well Lesson Notes

_____
_____
_____
_____
_____
_____
_____
_____
_____
_____
_____
_____

Today's Vocabulary

Words	Synonym	Antonym	Definition

Collocations/Phrases	Definition

What did I learn today?
_____
_____
_____
_____

What do I need to improve?
_____
_____
_____
_____

My homework for next class
_____
_____
_____

What is Ishin Denshin?

Warm Up

Classroom Discussion Questions
1. What Japanese cultural concepts should foreigners be aware of?
2. Whose feelings can you understand without them speaking?
3. Are you very good at hiding your feelings?
4. Are you good at reading between the lines?
5. How should foreigners interpret Japanese people silence at a meeting?
6. What gesture is very rude for Japanese?

Vocabulary Activity 1
Complete the sentences below with the phrases in the box.

| first impression | greatly prizes | visual signals |
| facial expressions | non-verbal communication | |

1. It is important to recognize that our _____ often speaks the loudest.
2. Our feelings of fear, anger, sadness, and happiness are often conveyed through our _____.
3. Sadly, our company _____ people who work long hours instead of those who are productive.
4. People are often unaware of the _____ they send.
5. A poor _____ can be nearly impossible to reverse or undo.

Vocabulary Activity 2
Complete the table with the words from the reading and their related forms

Noun	Verb	Adjective
communication		
	interpret	
	interact	
	strengthen	
impression		
reference		
		defensive
		receptive

Cultural Definitions
Define the following Japanese business terms and explain their importance to your classmate as if he or she was not Japanese.

Joshiki (常識)
_____
_____
_____

Hara o miseru (腹を 見せる)
_____
_____
_____

Myaku ari/myaku nashi (脈) (独創性)
_____
_____
_____

Gekokujo (下剋上)
_____
_____
_____

What is Ishin Denshin?

When people have lived together for a long time, they can start to communicate without words. They are exceedingly familiar with each other so they can easily communicate while using non-verbal communication. Non-verbal communication is not just body language but also includes tone of voice, personal space and the use of touch. It is an important part of communication in all cultures as it generally makes up 55 % of how people interact.

Ishin denshin is an expression that Japanese use to describe nonverbal communication. Some Japanese even believe that ishin denshin is a quasi-telepathic mutual understanding that they see as only existing between Japanese people. While the Japanese may have a word for nonverbal communication and prize it greatly, it is not unique to Japanese. Being a more homogenous culture than many, Japanese people have developed this ability, but so have other cultures such as Italian, Chinese, and Chilean.

American sociologist Edward T. Hall called these cultures high context cultures. In a higher-context culture, many things are left unsaid, as everyone within the culture possesses similar knowledge and understanding. The shared cultural knowledge explains what has not been said. .

However, relying on ishin denshin in cross-cultural meetings will not work. In cross-cultural communication situations, an individual will often have to explain him or herself in more detail and use stronger gestures. The cultural nonverbal references he or she relies on as part of ishin denshin do not exist in the other culture. Actions such as silence and lack of facial expressions may be misinterpreted as disinterest, coldness or apathy.

Japanese may have to speak more to convey their message than normal when talking to Westerners, but they have to remember that visual signals are still important. Even though someone is speaking, visual signals such as body language and facial expressions are being interpreted with equal importance.

Positive nonverbal communication can be an asset as if used correctly such as at dinner or in a business interview. Studies have found that first impressions are, on average formed within the first four seconds of contact. Therefore, in an initial meeting, a person should move in a way, he or she wishes to be seen.

In a meeting, body language will often tell others how you are feeling about the topic being discussed in the meeting. For Westerners, if a person is leaning away and slouching, it is a signal that they are bored or uninterested. While having arms folded across your front signals that the person probably will not be receptive to new ideas and is defensive. Different body language can have different interpretations in different lands.

People must remember when they speak a different language; they should change their body language. While speaking, gestures are very important as they can help increase the impact of their message. Studies have found that without gesturing, a speaker can lose his audience's attention. The wrong message can be received if the body language conveyed does not match the verbal message.

Instead, Japanese should talk more and use more expressive body language in not just meetings, but when speaking in English. Adapting body language and understanding other people's body language will give a person the ability to both pick up and send a message on another culture's wavelength, which will make him or her, a very effective communicator.

© David Baird

Ishin Denshin Activity Sheet

True and False Quiz
Based on the reading, circle whether the statements below are true or false.
1. Japanese people are telepathic. True/False
2. Ishin denshin is a Japanese expression for nonverbal communication. True/False
3. Arms folded across your chest shows you are thinking. True/False
4. The Japanese use of nonverbal communication is distinctive to only them. True/False
5. Depending on ishin denshin in meetings with foreigners will not succeed. True/False
6. All Westerners speak more to communicate than Japanese because they like to talk. True/False
7. When speaking a different language, people should try to change their gestures. True/False
8. Foreigners may think that silent Japanese do not care what someone is saying. True/False
9. Adapting your body language will give you ESP ability. True/False

Vocabulary Matching Activity
A. Match the words from the reading on the left with words of similar meaning on the right.

1. familiar   a) slumping
2. verbal   b) outlook
3. quasi   c) not caring
4. mutual   d) known
5. homogenous   e) shared
6. receptive   f) spoken
7. slouching   g) kind of
8. apathy   h) comprehend
9. pick up   i) open
10. wavelength   j) uniform

B. Now, choose four of the words from the above vocabulary exercise on the left side and write four sentences below using each of those words in a sentence.
   a) _____
   b) _____
   c) _____
   d) _____

Classroom Discussion Questions
Write discussion questions for class discussion based on the topic in the article. Next, ask your classmates your questions and make sure they give reasons.

   a) _____
   b) _____
   c) _____
   d) _____
   e) _____

Additional Questions for Discussion
Please discuss the questions below with your classmates. Ask your classmates follow up questions if needed. In addition, give detailed reasons to your answers.
1. How would you explain ishin denshin to a new arrival to Japan? What examples can you give?
2. What Japanese non-verbal communication do foreigners most misunderstand?
3. How does ishin denshin affect Japanese style of business?
4. Does ishin denshin affect negotiations?
5. In a 2010 survey concerning foreign co-workers, 50% of Japanese surveyed saw foreigners were not understanding ishin denshin as a liability in the workplace. Do you agree or disagree that it is a liability? Why?

Ishin Denshin Lesson Notes

_____
_____
_____
_____
_____
_____
_____
_____
_____
_____
_____

Today's Vocabulary

Words	Synonym	Antonym	Definition

Collocations/Phrases	Definition

What did I learn today?
_____
_____
_____
_____

What do I need to improve?
_____
_____
_____
_____

My homework for next class
_____
_____
_____
_____

© David Baird

Coffee and Doughnuts

Warm Up

Classroom Discussion Questions

Discuss the questions below with your classmates. Give your reasons.
1. What is your favorite snack? How often do you eat it?
2. How would you define good hospitality?
3. How do you make a visitor to your office feel welcome?
4. Are you a tea or coffee drinker? Do tea drinkers and coffee drinkers have different personalities?

Guess the Meaning Activity

Below are selected phrases from the reading. Working with a partner, create a definition.

1. standard fare   _____
2. their mind starts to wander   _____
3. quick high   _____
4. come down hard   _____
5. defeats the purpose   _____

Vocabulary Activity

Complete the table with the words from the reading and their related forms

Noun	Verb	Adjective
	sustain	
energy		
response		
		popular
tradition	XXXXXXX	
choice		
		sticky
		advisable

Collocation Activity

A. Match the verb with the noun that usually appears together.
Example: I *have time* in my schedule to study English.
Have time is a collocation

Verb	Noun/Adjective
get	a choice
fall	concentration
defeat	refreshments
lose	hungry
create	asleep
offer	a mess
make	the purpose

B. Now, write seven sentences using each of the above expressions.

a) _____
b) _____
c) _____
d) _____
e) _____
f) _____
g) _____

Coffee and Doughnuts

Now one can easily argue that coffee and doughnuts are very unhealthy foods, but coffee and doughnuts have become essential staples at many North American office meetings. Depending upon the country the savory snack may not always be a doughnut. For instance in France, it could be a croissant and in England, a Danish or scone. In many Western countries, offering some form of pastry or snack at a meeting is standard fare.

Why are snacks frequently offered at meetings? There are a few reasons for this unhealthy habit.

Firstly, people are often busy and may not have had time to have a proper meal, so the snack helps sustain them during the meeting. Which is important as people get hungry their mind starts to wander, and they lose concentration.

Next, people also lose energy while in a meeting, so the food is there to help them not fall asleep. Nevertheless, be careful as simple sugars from sweets can cause some people to have a quick high but then they will come down hard. After the initial sugar high, people will experience low blood sugar in response to the sweets, and the result is it will make them sleepy and weaken their concentration. This obviously defeats the purpose of why you gave them the sweets in the first place.

Finally, another reason for offering food comes from the tradition of being a good host. So when you are the chairperson remember that you are also the host of the meeting. A good host should offer food to their guests who are staying there for some time as this is good hospitality.

The best advice for meetings is to have an assortment of food, instead just having only Danishes, scones or doughnuts so the meeting participants can make a choice. In this day and age, some people are becoming more health conscious and because of allergies; fresh fruit should be included in the assortment. For drinks, while coffee and tea are the most popular beverages, there are some people who do not drink either. A good host should have some juice, soft drinks or bottled water available. Also, have serviettes and wet napkins on hand for people when their fingers may get sticky. No one wants to have smudged documents after a meeting.

Overall, the best course of action when offering savory treats depends upon the time and the purpose of the meeting. For instance, food would not be expected, if it were a short meeting. The general rule for when to have snacks available is for an early morning meeting, a meeting before lunch, close to dinner or late hours. In addition, the food should not create a mess, be noisy or difficult to eat. Given this criteria, dango, senbei and mochi would be inadvisable.

A chairperson has two roles, facilitator and host so serving snacks helps both roles. Refreshments help build a friendly relationship between participants and they will keep their minds focused on the meeting, as their stomachs are taken care of by delicious doughnuts and tasty coffee. By offering refreshments, the chairperson fulfills the primary function of a good host, which is seeing to the hospitality of guests.

© David Baird

Coffee and Doughnuts Activity Sheet

True and False Quiz
Based on the reading, circle whether the statements below are true or false.
1. Coffee and doughnuts are bad for people but are often offered at meetings. — True/False
2. In France, sponge cakes are usually offered at meetings. — True/False
3. Sweet snacks in meetings are good as they keep people awake. — True/False
4. People can become too keyed up when they eat too much sugar. — True/False
5. One sign of good hospitality is offering food to people. — True/False
6. Dango, senbei and mochi are ideal snacks to offer at a meeting. — True/False
7. Snacks are not usually anticipated at a brief meeting. — True/False
8. A meeting facilitator should have juice, wine, soft drinks or bottled water available for participants. — True/False
9. Having napkins on hand at a meeting is wise. — True/False

Vocabulary Matching Activity

A. Match the words from the reading on the left with words and phrases of similar meaning on the right

1) essential   a) reduce
2) staples   b) dirty
3) savory   c) napkins
4) wander   d) delicious
5) weaken   e) indispensable
6) high   f) buzzed or drunk
7) hospitality   g) popular or common food
8) conscious   h) aware
9) serviettes   i) sociability
10) smudged   j) roam

B. Now, choose five of the words from the above vocabulary exercise on the left and write five sentences below using each of those words in a sentence.
a) _____
b) _____
c) _____
d) _____
e) _____

Classroom Discussions Questions
Write questions for class discussions based on the topic in the article. Next, ask your classmates your questions and make sure they give reasons. Ask follow up questions if necessary.
a) _____
b) _____
c) _____
d) _____
e) _____

Additional Questions for Discussion
Please discuss the questions below with your classmates. Ask your classmates follow up questions if needed. In addition, give detailed reasons to your answers.
1. What advice would you give to keep a meeting interesting and attendees awake?
2. Are you a good host?
3. Do you mind people eating at business meetings?
4. What is your company's policy about eating in the office and at meetings?
5. Do you think being a bad host can ruin a meeting?
6. Do you take care about what you eat?
7. How do you stay awake in a boring meeting?
8. How do you keep other people awake in meetings?
9. Have you ever fallen asleep in a meeting? If yes, why did you fall asleep?
10. Have you ever seen anyone fall asleep in a meeting? If yes, how did other participants react?

Coffee and Doughnuts Lesson Notes

_____
_____
_____
_____
_____
_____
_____
_____
_____
_____
_____

Today's Vocabulary

Words	Synonym	Antonym	Definition

Collocations/Phrases	Definition

What did I learn today?
_____
_____
_____

What do I need to improve?
_____
_____
_____

My homework for next class
_____
_____
_____

No Is Not a Four Letter Word

Warm Up

Guessing the Definition Activity

A. Scan the reading and then try to guess what the following words and phrases mean.

Four-letter word _____
No-no _____
Play hardball _____
Once bitten, twice shy _____
Common courtesy _____
Bearer of bad news _____
Karma _____
Burn one's bridges _____

B. Choose four of the words or phrases on the left side from the above vocabulary exercise and write four sentences below using each of those words in a sentence.

a) _____
b) _____
c) _____
d) _____

Vocabulary Quiz

A. Choose words in each row that have a different meaning from the other words

1	numerous	countless	plentiful	scarce	bountiful
2	harmonious	melodious	pleasant	corresponding	discordant
3	potential	possible	unattainable	prospective	budding
4	optimistic	hopeful	cheerful	confident	negative
5	bitter	mild	sharp	angry	harsh
6	deceptive	suitable	legitimate	sound	valid
7	discreet	tactful	inconsiderate	careful	diplomatic

Bad or Good Rejection Phrases Activity

The phrases below are phrases to express no. Classify them in the columns below into bad or good rejection phrases.

Let me get back to you after I have discussed it with management.
This doesn't meet our needs now, but we'll be sure to keep you in mind.

We have considered your proposal, but we're sorry to say we don't have the budget.
We will agree when hell freezes over.
We are open to the idea, so please let us study it

I'm sorry, but we have decided to limit our commitments as the market has changed.
We found your bid well prepared, but higher than the other bids, so we have rewarded the contract to another firm.
There are many good options for us, yours is not one of them.
I'm afraid we can't possibly support that
We appreciate your offer and we'll contact you for other projects, but we are going a different way.

Bad Rejection Phrases	Good Rejection Phrases

No Is Not a Four Letter Word

Many people have a difficult time saying no. There are numerous reasons why so many people have a hard time saying no. They could be passive; afraid of hurting people' feelings; do not want to be in an uncomfortable situation; enjoy being the "Go To" person when problems arise, etc. However, these people can check out the numerous websites, self-help books and counselors that teach people to disagree, to refuse or deny.

In Japanese business, saying no is a big no-no. Why? Because no causes conflict and disrupts the harmony, the *wa* (和) and saying it causes a loss of face. This belief often results in a Japanese company delaying stating anything for such a long time, so that whoever is dealing with them will walk away exasperated. The counterparty if approached again will be wary, cautious and eager to play hardball at the next bargaining session. Once bitten, twice shy.

Think of a business relationship as dating. Imagine the scenario of a young man just after a first date and is analyzing whether the first date was successful or not. The girl sounded positive and seemed interested in continuing the relationship, so he is optimistic, believing there will be a second date and a romantic relationship will develop. He waits and there is no call back. He calls her, but she is evasive about a second date.

After some time, she does not even answer his calls. Then he moves on to the next stage and starts to get angry at their romantic interest for not having the decency to call back. Could the person at least have the good manners to call? After all, it is just common courtesy and a need for a little social honesty. Finally, the young man tries to forget the whole experience over time but a bitter memory will always remain.

Japanese should remember this scenario in their business dealings with foreigners. For while saying no may put the person responsible in an uncomfortable situation and disturb his *wa*, it does not create a harmonious relationship with a potential business partner. While they may not be a suitable business partner now, they could be in the future. A polite refusal is usually a professional and respectful thing to do and does not give false hope to the vendor.

By not saying no in a timely manner, then the counterparts probably feel their time has been wasted. Remember in business, the often-quoted maxim, time is money. Therefore, by wasting their time, they now feel their Japanese opposite has wasted their money.

Now some Japanese business people will argue against this need for a change in style as foreign business people should adjust to the country they are doing business in. When in Rome, do as Romans do. These critics have a valid point, but they should remember that the Japanese market is no longer as attractive as it once was. An excellent vendor can find another client, not just in Japan, but can move onto China, India, and Southeast Asia.

So how does one say no in business? Instead of negotiations and discussions ending with a shrug and a vague statement, perhaps adopting the cooperative negotiating style promoted by the Harvard Negotiation Project. They advise people to be honest, share information and describe what the entire process will entail so counterparts will understand all the details and obstacles that exist. By creating a partnership built on trust and transparency, then a harmonious relationship can be built.

Finally, a person should just imagine how they would like to be told no. Most business people prefer a professional, discreet and respectful manner. Additionally, the bearer of bad news should be clear and give valid reasons for the rejection, refusal or disagreement.

Buyers should not ignore karma, for that what is given whether bad or good is what is received at the end. One day that rejected supplier might be desperately needed for a new project, so do not burn any bridges.

© David Baird

No Is Not a Four Letter Word Activity Sheet

True and False Quiz
Based on the reading, circle whether the statements below are true or false.
1. People do not say no because they are timid or worried about hurting people's feelings — True/ False
2. In Japanese business, saying no is a big taboo. — True/ False
3. Young men often have fond memories of girls rejecting them. — True/ False
4. All Japanese business people believe that when in Rome, do as Romans do. — True/ False
5. A polite refusal frequently causes shame and embarrassment. — True/ False
6. Japan is still an attractive market for many companies. — True/ False
7. The Harvard Negotiation Project encourages a cooperative negotiating style. — True/ False
8. The person who rejects someone should give clear reasons. — True/ False
9. According to the concept of karma, you will receive the opposite of what you give. — True/ False

Vocabulary Matching Activity
A. Match the words on the left from the reading with the synonyms or meanings on the right

1. passive
2. check out
3. exasperated
4. analyzing
5. evasive
6. opposite
7. decency
8. cooperative
9. entails
10. transparency

a) civility
b) mutual
c) involves
d) openness
e) counterpart
f) timid
g) review
h) elusive
i) frustrated
j) scrutinizing

B. Choose five of the words from the above vocabulary exercise on the left and write five sentences below using each of those words in a sentence. You may change the form of the words.

a) _____
b) _____
c) _____
d) _____
e) _____

Classroom Discussion Questions
Write discussion questions for class discussions based on the topic in the article. Next, ask your classmates your questions and make sure they give reasons.

a) _____
b) _____
c) _____
d) _____

Additional Questions for Discussion
Please discuss the questions below with your classmates. Ask your classmates follow up questions if needed. In addition, give detailed reasons to your answers.

1. Are you good at saying no?
2. Is saying no a big no-no in your culture?
3. What is *wa* and why is it important?
4. How do you get over rejection?
5. When in Rome, should you do as Romans do?
6. Do you believe that negotiations can be cooperative?
7. How would you build a harmonious relationship?
8. Do you believe in karma?

No Is Not a Four Letter Word Lesson Notes

Today's Vocabulary

Words	Synonym	Antonym	Definition

Collocations/Phrases	Definition

What did I learn today?

What do I need to improve?

My homework for next class

Ambiguity, Vagueness and the Unknown
Warm Up

Classroom Discussion Questions
1. What is the greatest mystery in the universe?
2. What scientific discovery has amazed you?
3. How do you deal with things you observe that you cannot explain?
4. Are you comfortable when work becomes uncertain?

Vocabulary Finding Activity
A. Find words in the article that mean
1. puzzles   _____
2. prehistoric   _____
3. legends   _____
4. overall view   _____
5. succinctly   _____
6. nuance   _____
7. deliberate   _____
8. aggravation   _____
9. point out   _____
10. unfeeling   _____

B. Now, choose five of the words that you have found in the article from the above vocabulary exercise and write five sentences below using each of those words in a sentence.
a) _____
b) _____
c) _____
d) _____

Grammar Activity
Put in the proper preposition in each of the phrases below.

between	by	in	of	into

1. surrounded _____ the unknown
2. reading _____ the lines
3. divided _____ two types
4. feeling _____ frustration
5. fills _____ the gaps

Writing Activity
Compare your culture and another culture that you are familiar with and write how they are similar and how are they different?

_____
_____
_____
_____
_____
_____
_____
_____
_____
_____
_____
_____
_____
_____

Ambiguity, Vagueness and the Unknown

For thousands of years people have wondered about how and why the universe started, how old the Earth is and where did humanity come from. Primitive man answered these questions by creating gods and myths to explain these mysteries. In the last six hundred years, scientists have made great strides in unlocking the secrets of the universe.

While the mysteries of the universe are slowly being explained, people are still surrounded by another constant unknown, other people. When we interact with people, we often do not know how they will react. What exactly are they thinking? What did they mean when they said "..."? What does my boss exactly want me to do? What was my co-worker implying?

Reading between the lines is difficult for all people, but for some people even more so. Each culture according to some social scientists tolerates ambiguity differently. Some cultures find intentional vagueness to be quite frustrating and a sign of indecisiveness, while other cultures are more accepting and see ambiguous communication as a style to maintain harmony.

The noted American anthropologist Edward T. Hall divided cultures into two types, high context and low context culture. In general, people in a high context culture share many similar experiences and have a group mentality. This culture creates a communication style where many things are left unsaid, since a few words can communicate a complex message very effectively to the in-group. The widely shared cultural knowledge fills in the gaps between the lines.

Conversely, the low context culture is more individualistic, so the communicator needs to explain concisely that make messages direct. Communication is for exchanging information, ideas, and opinions. Low context people want and need detailed background information to understand the big picture and how everything fits.

Even within different cultures, there are variances. For example, while Japan is described as being a high context culture there are variances within Japan. Kyoto people would be considered high context types while Osaka natives are comparatively low context.

When people from low context cultures meet with people from high context cultures, the outcomes can be uneven and sometimes strained. The low context individual can interpret the terse responses from the high context culture many different ways. He may think they are interested because they said nothing negative or not interested at all because they did not make any definite commitments. The end result for the low context person is a feeling of frustration as they are not experienced with dealing with ambiguity.

For the high context person, low-context people seem insensitive, tactless and inharmonious by directly dealing with issues. Moreover, they are seen as impatient and lacking subtlety. High context people want everyone to take the time to establish relationships and understand the context before decisions are made.

For a low context person working in a high context culture, the best advice is to be patient, concentrate on building relationships and discuss things privately, not in a group discussion. High context individuals should be prepared to interrupt and articulate problems early. Finally be prepared to say no quickly and politely, so the low context person will not feel like they have been wasting their time.

Even with all this high-context and low-context analysis of behavior, it is easy for people to peg people's behavior on where they are from. However, that would be a trap as there are many other factors that influence individual behavior such as family, friends and education that can be more powerful than culture in influencing behavior.

© David Baird

Ambiguity, the Vagueness and the Unknown Activity Sheet

True and False Quiz
Based on the reading, circle whether the statements below are true or false.

1. Primitive man believed that gods created uncertainties to confuse people. — True/ False
2. Reading between the lines is difficult for all people, but easier for Japanese. — True/ False
3. High context communication style is not very wordy. — True/ False
4. People from Kyoto are low context while Osaka natives are high context. — True/ False
5. Low context people can never adapt to high context environments. — True/ False
6. High context culture individuals view low-context people as insensitive and tactless. — True/ False
7. After a meeting between low and high context groups, low-context people are often happy with the results. — True/ False
8. Low context people should be very demanding in meetings with high-context people in order to get the best results. — True/ False
9. Culture is the primary factor that influences people's behavior. — True/ False

Vocabulary Matching Activity
A. Match the words on the left from the reading with the synonyms or meanings on the right

1) ambiguity   a) relate
2) strides   b) uncertainty
3) interact   c) differences
4) implying   d) inconsiderate
5) fits   e) tense
6) tolerates   f) advances
7) variances   g) meshes
8) terse   h) categorize
9) strained   i) accepts
10) tactless   j) brief or curt
11) peg   k) meaning

B. Now, choose five of the words on the left from the above vocabulary exercise and write five sentences below using each of those words in a sentence. . You may change the form of the words.

a) _____
b) _____
c) _____
d) _____
e) _____

Classroom Discussion Questions
Please discuss the questions below with your classmates. Give detailed answers.

1) How do you deal when situations at work become uncertain and ambiguous?
2) What are your views on the high-context and low-context culture theory?
3) Do you consider yourself to be direct when you communicate?
4) Have you ever been confused by high-context behavior? Low-context behavior?
5) What do you think influences people's behavior the most?
6) What is your opinion of people from Osaka's communications style?
7) What advice would you give to a low context person employed at a high context culture company?

Write four questions for class discussions based on the topic in the article. Next, ask your classmates your questions and make sure they give reasons.

a) _____
b) _____
c) _____
d) _____

Ambiguity, Vagueness and the Unknown
Lesson Notes

Today's Vocabulary

Words	Synonym	Antonym	Definition

Collocations/Phrases	Definition

What did I learn today?

What do I need to improve?

My homework for next class

Looking in the Mirror

Warm Up

What Do You Know about Japan?
1. Who is Nigo?
2. Name a movie that Akira Kurosawa directed?
3. When was instant ramen invented?
4. Name three Japanese Nobel Prizes winners?
5. Which company introduced flash memory?
6. What is the Deming Prize for?

Classroom Discussion Questions
1. How do Japanese describe themselves?
2. What do you think is Japan's greatest invention?
3. Who do you think is the most creative person in Japan?
4. What do you think is the most creative Japanese company?

Vocabulary Finding Activity
A. Scan the article and find words that have a similar meaning to the words on the left.
1. modifiers
2. dependability
3. prominent
4. notion
5. direction
6. bring up to date
7. trying out
8. help

B. Now, choose four of the words you found in the article in the above activity and write four sentences below using each of those words in a sentence.
a)
b)
c)
d)

Business Vocabulary Matching Activity
Match the following business terms with their definitions on the right

1. Quality assurance
2. Quality control
3. Margin
4. Quality Improvement

a) This activity emphasizes testing of products to uncover defects before selling
b) A formal approach to the analysis of performance and systematic efforts to make it better. Examples are TQM and Six Sigma.
c) An administrative and procedural system to ensure a good meets certain requirements.
d) The difference between revenue and cost before accounting for certain other costs.

Summarize the Article
Read the article and summarize it in three sentences.

Looking in the Mirror

The Japanese perceive themselves as great adapters of technology, but not creators. Furthermore, their globally respected products are known for high quality and reliability is the result of companies following the Japanese way of doing things.

This widely held belief does not hold up when examined more closely. Since 1949, Japan has produced over 18 Noble Prize winners in medicine, chemistry, physics and literature. In fashion, Japan has world-class designers from Issey Miyuke and Michiko Koshino to hip-hop designer Nigo. Japanese have contributed to popular culture with its manga and anime having worldwide fans. Filmmakers such as Akira Kurosawa, Takeshi Kitano and Yojiro Takita have been honored at the world's most prestigious film festivals. Japanese have also given the world flash memory, karaoke, instant ramen, video games, pocket calculators, blue ray discs, CD players, etc. Yet for all this creativity, the Japanese do not see themselves as original, inventive or creative.

The other part of the perception, that Japanese companies used Japanese methods to be successful, is also not exactly accurate. After WWII, when Japan was rebuilding and the economy was more open, the government and industry did not look inside for help, but instead went outside inviting American management experts to advise them.

While there were many experts who gave lectures and guidance, there were three in particular who had a great impact on Japanese business, Peter Drucker, Joseph Juran and W. Edwards Deming. Each of these management gurus' advice helped Japanese manufacturers evolve from producers of cheap second-rate products to global leaders who produced quality goods. Their teachings strongly impacted how the Japanese approached management, production, quality assurance and quality control.

Peter Drucker's advice helped modernize Japanese modern management to focus on clear and measurable goals. He urged Japanese managers to brace for competition by working out what they were good at, what they should not do and what their values were. Drucker's ideas have become popular again in Japan thanks to the manga, "What If the Manageress of a High School Baseball Team Read Drucker's "Management?"

Joseph Juran focused on managing for quality with a cross-functional management approach. He pushed companies to train their managers for quality planning, improving quality control and making quality improvement a priority. He saw eliminating constant waste as a way to decrease costs and to create higher margins over the long run. The higher margins would recoup the initial costs incurred by creating high standard quality control and assurance departments.

W. Edwards Deming, the last but not the least, was also concerned about quality control but his approach was more statistically based yet incorporated people as a major component. He emphasized on solving problems through cooperation and saw marketing as a science where companies should know why customers buy a product and whether they will buy it again. Additionally a company must apply statistical techniques for experimenting, planning and inspection of samples. Finally, the company should perfect its manufacturing process.

The Japanese government and Japanese industry honored all of these men for their contribution and assistance in helping Japan become a leading industrial nation. Yet years after their contribution, many Japanese have become insular and have forgotten that Japanese looked outside to change the way they approached business, management and manufacturing. Perhaps it is time for Japanese leaders to take another look outside.

© David Baird

Looking in the Mirror Activity Sheet

True and False Quiz
Based on the reading, circle whether the statements below are true or false
1. Japanese see themselves as very creative and inventive. — True/False
2. Japan has more than 20 Noble Prize winners. — True/False
3. After WWII, Japanese business people were more receptive to ideas originating from outside Japan. — True/False
4. A manga was made about Peter Drucker's life in Japan. — True/False
5. Japanese listened to Peter Drucker's advice but did not follow it. — True/False
6. Joseph Juran pushed companies to train their managers. — True/False
7. Deming used statistics as a way to analyze quality control. — True/False
8. Japanese business people seldom look outside Japan these days. — True/False

Vocabulary Matching Activity
A. Match the words from the reading on the left with the words that have a similar meaning from the words on the right

1. contributed   a. substandard
2. accurate   b. multi-departmental
3. gurus   c. inward-looking
4. second rate   d. get back
5. cross-functional   e. reducing
6. eliminating   f. gave
7. recoup   g. true
8. insular   h. experts

B. Now, choose four of the words on the left side from the above vocabulary exercise and write four sentences below using each of those words in a sentence.
a) _____
b) _____
c) _____
d) _____

Reading Comprehension Activity
For each pair of statements below decide which one is the most accurate.
1. a. Akira Kurosawa, Takeshi Kitano and Yojiro Takita have all won Oscars.
   b. Akira Kurosawa, Takeshi Kitano and Yojiro Takita have received awards at prestigious film festivals
2. a. Of the three experts mentioned, W. Edward Deming is now the most well known.
   b. Of the three experts mentioned, W. Edward Deming had the greatest impact.
3. a. Juran focused on managing for quality with a multi-departmental management approach.
   b. Juran focused on improving management so greater margins would result.

Classroom Discussion Questions
Write five questions for class discussion based on the topic in the article. Next, ask your classmates your questions and make sure they give reasons.
a) _____
b) _____
c) _____
d) _____
e) _____

Additional Questions for Discussion
Please discuss the questions below with your classmates. Give detailed answers.
2. Do you think Japanese people are creative?
3. If you wanted to make young people more creative, how would you do it?
4. If you wanted to make your company's employees more creative, how would you do it?
5. What do you know of Peter Drucker, Joseph Juran and W. Edward Deming?
6. Should Japanese business people look abroad for new ideas?
7. How would you revitalize Japan?

Looking in the Mirror Lesson Notes

_____
_____
_____
_____
_____
_____
_____
_____
_____
_____
_____
_____

Today's Vocabulary

Words	Synonym	Antonym	Definition

Collocations/Phrases	Definition

What did I learn today?
_____
_____
_____
_____

What do I need to improve?
_____
_____
_____
_____

My homework for next class
_____
_____
_____

Cross-Cultural Vocabulary Review

Vocabulary Review A
Fill in the blanks in the following passages with the words below.

    anecdotes   impression   follow-up   firm
        expressions   wander   smile

    When meeting someone for the first time, it is important to make a good first _____. .The first thing is to be friendly, smile and give a _____ handshake and say your name slowly and clearly.
    During the conversation, ask _____ questions and have attentive body language. Do not spend all the time telling your new acquaintance about some personal _____ or gossip, but get them talking. Be careful about your facial _____ and don't let your mind _____.

    obstacle   hospitality   interact
    conglomerates   strides   attract

    The Japanese government wants Japan to become one of the top tourist destinations in Asia but for the _____ industry, this is a challenge. Hotels face the _____ of finding staff that are confident, skilled and poised in dealing with guests from around the world. For the major hotel _____ such as the Ritz or the Hyatt, this is no problem as they have the resources to _____ such staff. Nevertheless, for the second tier chains and independent operators this is not so easy. They will have to make great _____ in improving their hotel's staff language skills if they want their guests to _____ well and feel at home during their stay.

Vocabulary Review B
Choose the best word to complete the sentences.
1. Beans and corn are the main (staples/stables) of the Mexican diet.
2. The best (healing/cure) for the common cold is sleep, rest and drinking plenty of fluids.
3. He caused many problems as he was seldom (unaware/conscious) of how his remarks hurt people.
4. My boss and I are hardly ever on the same (book/wavelength) so we don't get along.
5. He needed to (adopt/adjust) his estimates because he didn't include a possible rise in oil prices.
6. As she always eats at her desk, her paperwork always has (smudges/smuggles).
7. He is not (capable/familiar) of managing so many people.
8. They say young people are (interested/apathetic) so that is why few of them vote.

Writing Review
Answer one of the following questions in the space provided below. Make sure to give details and supporting reasons.
1. What do you think is the greatest mystery in the universe?
2. What scientific discovery has amazed you?
3. Which is better, coffee or tea?
4. What advice would you give a foreigner starting a business in Japan?

_____
_____
_____
_____
_____
_____
_____
_____
_____
_____
_____

Cross-Culture Articles Vocabulary Review

Wonderword Puzzle

Answer all the clues for the words in the columns below. Many words are from the previous units. The words are also in the box of letters below. The clues are synonyms, collocations, idioms, sayings or titles.

1. Real __ __ t h __ __ __ __ c
2. Standard *fare*
3. Uncertainty a m __ __ __ __ __ __ y
4. Discretion __ __ c t
5. Curt __ e __ r __ __
6. Fundamental __ a s __ __
7. Pigeonhole __ __ __ g
8. Words cannot __ e __ s __ r __ your beauty.
9. Awkward __ l u __ __ __ y
10. Tokyo's __ u __ __ __ r is hot and humid.
11. Put it another way __ e __ __ __ s e
12. Delicious __ a __ v __ __ __
13. "A __ __ v __ __ r Runs Through It" Brad Pitt movie
14. Daifuku mochi, caramel and peanut butter are all __ t __ __ k __ y
15. Legend __ y __ __ h
16. Fantastic __ a b __ __ __ __ s
17. Elegant __ r __ c __ __ __ l
18. Try __ __ __ for the team
19. Do not take no for an answer. __ n s __ __ __ t
20. Defeats the __ u __ p __ __
21. Reboot r __ __ __ __ t
22. Leave out __ m __ i __
23. Q __ __ __ k and easy meals are great.
24. Help a __ __ i __ __ __ __ __ c e
25. Proficiency d __ __ x __ __ __ __ __ t
26. Pseudo __ u __ s __
27. Many Chinese dissidents were put under house __ r r __ __ t.
28. Prominent __ r e __ __ __ __ __ __ s
29. __ u __ __ rman is from Krypton
30. Details __ a __ t __ __
31. Prehistoric p r __ __ __ i v __
32. Spoken v __ __ __ b __ __ __
33. Bible Ark builder N __ __ __ __
34. __ __ t t __ -Frutti (Little Richard song)
35. Aim __ o __ __ __
36. Holy __ a __ __ r __ d
37. Cuban Dance __ h __ m __ a
38. The __ __ q __ __ __ __ k __ y wheel gets the grease.
39. The largest deer __ o __ s __ e
40. Drift m __ __ __ n __ __ r
41. Understand __ __ a __ s __
42. I D __ __ __ v __ All Night (Cyndi Lauper song)
43. Second – r __ __ __ __
44. I'm not important so I have a very __ i __ __ __ office in the basement. It's 2 meters by 2 meters.
45. An elegant dance __ a __ __ __ e t
46. Ticket s __ __ __ b

Step Two

All the words in the columns above appear in the box below. When you find a word, circle it. The words can be vertical, horizontal or diagonal. There will be ten letters, still remaining. Unscramble those letters to spell the wonder word phrase.

F	A	R	E	P	H	R	A	S	E	A	P	F
S	U	M	M	E	R	P	R	U	G	S	R	A
S	T	U	B	I	P	U	R	P	O	S	E	B
D	H	B	A	I	E	C	E	E	A	I	S	U
T	E	R	S	E	G	L	S	R	L	S	T	L
I	N	S	I	S	T	U	T	T	T	T	I	O
G	T	A	C	T	O	M	I	T	I	A	G	U
R	I	V	E	R	E	S	E	T	N	N	I	S
A	C	O	U	T	I	Y	T	R	Y	C	O	A
C	M	R	H	U	M	B	A	I	A	E	U	C
E	E	Y	I	C	O	G	E	U	C	T	S	R
F	A	C	T	S	O	Q	U	I	C	K	E	E
U	N	O	A	H	S	Q	U	E	A	K	Y	D
L	D	R	O	V	E	R	B	A	L	L	E	T
D	E	X	T	E	R	I	T	Y	S	R	T	E
G	R	A	S	P	R	I	M	I	T	I	V	E

Wonder Word Phrase (hint book title) The __ __ __   __ __ __ __ __ __ __ __

Cross-Culture Articles Review

Discussion Questions

How do you define culture?
How would you define cultural diversity?
How do your gender and class define you?
What is a cultural stereotype? Give an example of 2-3 stereotypes/prejudice that find other cultures have about your culture. Explain the reasons for the stereotyped behavior/activity/feeling/event to your classmates.
Give an example from your own culture that someone from another culture might have difficulty understanding.
What would you request from members of another culture to help you communicate better with them?
Can you interact effectively with people from different cultures?
Discuss the types of communication problems that have occurred when you have interacted with people from cultures different than your own. Describe what happened and explain how these difficulties made you feel.

What Have You Learned So Far?

Write your thoughts on what the most interesting, most surprising, most controversial topic that you have discussed from the Cross-Cultural Section.

People Discussion Articles

Another Day in the Rat Race

Warm Up

Classroom Discussion Questions
1) Do animals have personalities like people?
2) Have you ever owned a pet? If yes, describe its personality?
3) Explain an animal idiom from your own language in English to your classmates. Teach them how to use it.
4) If someone were described as a cockroach, what would you think that person was like?

Animal Personality Activity
What personality traits would you imagine the following animals have?
Example: monkey: mischievous, clever, friendly, fun-loving, curious, entertaining

Snake _____
Shark _____
Poodle _____
Tiger _____
Horse _____
Bear _____
Sheep _____

Animal Idiom Match Activity

A. Match the words from the left column with the words from the right to create some common idioms.

night	cow	Night Owl_____
monkey	in the grass	_____
early	doghouse	_____
bull	out	_____
dog and	owl	_____
cry	kitten	_____
snake	pony show	_____
pig	wolf	_____
as weak as a	bird	_____
cash	business	_____
in the	market	_____

B. Now, choose five of the idioms from the above vocabulary exercise on the left side and write five sentences below using each of those idioms in a sentence.
1. _____
2. _____
3. _____
4. _____
5. _____

Animal Idiom Discussion Questions
Write three questions for class discussions using one of the above animal idioms in each of the questions.

a) _____
b) _____
c) _____

© David Baird

Another Day in the Rat Race

It's another day in the rat race where you're getting chickenfeed yet working like a dog. Your competitors are sharks, your boss is a dinosaur and your coworker is a snake while another is a pig. Your subordinates cannot stop monkeying around while they try to weasel out of work. When you have a meeting, everyone acts like sheep while the meeting goes at a snail's pace. What your office really needs is everyone to be a hive of worker bees and have some workhorses.

From the above complaints, you may think that you are working in a zoo not in an office. However, for native speakers they would understand that you are working in an office, albeit a dysfunctional one. In English, as in many languages, animals are often used in metaphors, similes and idioms to describe personalities and people's actions. Some have positive attributes while others have negative meanings. How these traits and attributes are assigned to various animals comes from a selection of sources such as folklore, nursery rhymes and literature.

Certain animals are almost universally given negative attributes such as snakes or vultures. People probably loathe snakes since man's initial contact with snakes was not pleasant as its venomous bites caused many deaths. With their appearance, their behavior and their deadly characteristics, people associate them with evil. In Christianity, the devil disguised as a snake is responsible for humanity's expulsion from paradise.

Some psychologists have hypothesized that our collective unconscious is responsible for people's continued fear of snakes as most people seldom encounter snakes. Therefore, if someone is described as a snake, the person is usually sneaky and despised. If they are a snake in the grass, then they are someone who will cause you trouble yet you will never see their attack coming or they are a false friend.

Other animals that are never used as compliments are cockroaches, donkeys, gorillas, vultures and rats. Strangely, the dog, which has been humankind's companion for over 15,000 years, is used in both positive and negative expressions. To call a person a dog may occasionally imply a positive trait, but more often, the person is regarded as contemptible, ugly or dull. If something is a dog then it could be of low quality or in business a bad investment.

Probably the horse, which has been an important animal in humanity's development, is more often used in positive English expressions than negative ones. You should have horse sense (common sense), be a workhorse (hard worker) and healthy as a horse (be very healthy). For a man being a stallion means you are virile and very attractive to women. Still you should never tell a person that they look like a horse because that would be an insult.

What is a student to do? Are there just too many idioms and expressions for students to learn? In short, yes there are. There are so many idioms and expressions that even most native speakers do not know them all. However, idioms are commonly used in everyday conversation by native English speakers and are an important cultural element of the language.

To understand a native speaker and sound like one, you should learn some idioms. When you see or hear a new idiom or expression then you should try to integrate it into your speech so it will sound more interesting, natural and expressive.

© David Baird

Another Day in the Rat Race Activity Sheet

True and False Quiz
Based on the reading, circle whether the statements below are true or false.
1. An office needs to have jackals and snakes. True/False
2. Animals are often used in metaphors, similes and idioms to describe people's attributes. True/False
3. Snakes are well loved in most societies. True/False
4. Snakes causing the death of many people is the reason most people hate them. True/False
5. Animals that can be used as insults are cockroaches, donkeys, gorillas, vultures and rats. True/False
6. The dog is predominantly used in positive idioms. True/False
7. The horse is primarily used in positive idioms. True/False
8. Students should not learn idioms because there are too many to learn. True/False

Vocabulary Matching Activity
A. Match the words from the article on the left with the synonyms and definitions on the right.

1. rat race
2. chickenfeed
3. pig
4. shark
5. dinosaur
6. traits
7. albeit
8. collective unconscious
9. despised
10. vultures
11. contemptible

a) attributes
b) hated
c) frustrating, hard-to-break even lifestyle
d) despicable
e) ruthless competitor
f) someone who preys upon weaker people
g) poor pay
h) out of date thinker
i) although
j) greedy or dirty person
k) ancestral memory that is common to all

B. Now, choose five of the words from the left column and write sentences below using each one in a sentence.
a) _____
b) _____
c) _____
d) _____
e) _____

Classroom Discussion Questions
Discuss the questions below with your classmates. Give your reasons.
1. What animal would you describe yourself as? Why?
2. Do you feel like you work in the rat race?
3. Who do you think is a dinosaur?
4. How often do you try to weasel out of work?
5. Do you get frustrated when things go at a snail's pace? What is your reaction?
6. Have you ever had to deal with a snake?
7. Do people in your office act like sheep?
8. Are there any animals you would be afraid to encounter?
9. Do idioms confuse you when you first hear them? What is your strategy to understand and remember them?
10. What English idiom have you enjoyed learning and using?

Write discussion questions for class discussions based on the topic in the article. Try to use the idioms from this article in your questions.
a) _____
b) _____
c) _____
d) _____

Another Day in the Rat Race Lesson Notes

_____
_____
_____
_____
_____
_____
_____
_____
_____
_____
_____
_____

Today's Vocabulary

Words	Synonym	Antonym	Definition

Collocations/Phrases	Definition

What did I learn today?
_____
_____
_____

What do I need to improve?
_____
_____
_____

My homework for next class
_____
_____
_____

© David Baird

The Fourth Type

Warm Up

How Assertive Are You?

Answer the questions below honestly. They will help you gain some insights about your current level of assertiveness.

Assign a number to each item using this scale:

Always   5   4   3   2   1   Never

_____	I ask others to do things without feeling guilty or anxious.
_____	When someone asks me to do something I don't want to do, I say "no" without feeling guilty or anxious.
_____	I am comfortable when speaking to a large group of people.
_____	I confidently express my honest opinions to authority figures.
_____	When I experience powerful feelings (anger, frustration, disappointment, etc.), I verbalize them easily.
_____	When I express anger, I do so without blaming others for "making me mad."
_____	I am comfortable speaking up in a group situation.
_____	If I disagree with the majority opinion in a meeting, I can "stick to my guns" without feeling uncomfortable or being abrasive.
_____	When I make a mistake, I acknowledge it.
_____	I can tell others when their behavior creates a problem for me.
_____	Meeting new people in social situations is something I do with ease and comfort.
_____	When discussing my beliefs, I do so without labeling the opinions of others as "crazy," "stupid," "ridiculous," or irrational."
_____	I assume that most people are competent and trustworthy and do not have difficulty delegating tasks to others.
_____	When considering doing something I have never done, I feel confident I can learn to do it.
_____	I believe my needs are as important as those of others and I am entitled to have my needs satisfied
_____	**Total Score**

Classroom Discussion Questions

1. How do you deal with confrontation?
2. How would you describe your behavior?
3. Do you know anyone who is aggressive? How do you deal with them?
4. Do you know anyone who is passive? How do you deal with them?

How Do You Deal with It?

With a classmate, write down the best solution on how to deal with these problems.

1. An associate sends you very blunt, almost rude e-mails but when you see them in person, they act very friendly.
   _____

2. A co-worker procrastinates every time you make a request. He agrees to do it but then delays completing the work until the very last moment, or worse hands it in late.
   _____

3. You are working on a project. A colleague withholds important information from the rest of the team so she can appear more important and more valuable and the rest of the team looks bad.
   _____
   _____

The Fourth Type

Many psychologists label people's behavior into four types based on how they communicate in relationships; aggressive, assertive, passive and passive- aggressive. Aggressive and passive are easy to understand and identify. Assertiveness is being self-assured and confident without being aggressive and is a behavioral skill taught the most in business.

However, what is this fourth type, passive-aggressive behavior? How can someone be both aggressive and passive at the same time? It is not uncommon for people to express anger in a passive or indirect way. For example, the passive aggressive individual will pretend agreement with plans but will express antagonism through procrastination, stubbornness, complaining, or deliberate failure of assigned tasks.

A US Army psychiatrist first coined the term in WWII. He applied it to soldiers who did not openly disobey orders but expressed their aggressiveness passively by being sullen, stubborn, and inefficient. Additional behavior now associated with passive-aggressive behavior is performing a task poorly, a cynical attitude, feeling underappreciated, and not speaking up when someone else is going to make a serious mistake. Additionally, they insist on seeing themselves as the blameless victims in all situations

At various times, many people may have difficulty expressing negative feelings, so they use passive aggressive behavior. That does not mean they are mentally ill. Passive – aggressiveness is a personality disorder but many people exhibit the characteristics of possessing of it at one time, or another. A personality disorder such as passive-aggressive behavior only becomes a serious problem when it hinders someone's ability to have healthy personal relationships or to function in society

Of course, this behavior can be identified by people's actions but also by the words they use. If you frequently hear words and phrases coming from someone such as I'll try, if, whatever, maybe, kind of..., I don't know, I'll get back to you, you might be ..., Yes, but ... and I guess ..., then you have probably encountered someone with passive aggressive behavior. All of those phrases are okay to use and everyone uses them at some time. However, if you are hearing, "I'll get back to you" over and over again when you are asking for a project update, you are now receiving a sign that you are probably dealing with a passive-aggressive personality.

The strongest passive-aggressive signal that often causes the worst reaction is the word *whatever*. Many people consider this a rude and dismissive expression to end a discussion. If someone responds to something, with "Whatever" then listeners will see the reply as contempt for the conversation and for whom it was addressed to.

Oddly, most psychologists do not often discuss the situation of a passive-aggressive manager. This type of manager rarely gives any critique concerning work performance, has vague and unnecessary rules, cares more for trivial details and avoids sharing what he knows at all costs. The best advice for an employee in that situation is to simply focus on your work environment, don't put much stake in how your boss behaves from one moment to the next, and look elsewhere for professional development.

The indirectness of Japanese culture and business has caused some foreigners to consider Japanese as being passive-aggressive. While confrontation and directly saying no are not part of Japanese culture, some foreigners wrongly misinterpret it as passive aggressive behavior. If Japanese want to have a harmonious relationship with foreign business associates, they may wish to alter their style and be more direct.

Within all cultures, people have to deal with passive-aggressive personalities as they are just one of the many types of people. You probably cannot change them, but just do not allow them to affect you. Additionally have a Plan B, as passive-aggressives do not often keep their promises. After learning how to deal with passive aggressive types, you will find that your life as well as having to deal with them much easier.

© David Baird

The Fourth Type Activity Sheet

True or False Quiz
Based on the reading, circle whether the statements are true or false.
1. Various psychologists label people into four types of personalities. True/False
2. Numerous people often express anger in a passive or indirect way. True/False
3. Examples of passive-aggressive behavior are stubbornness, complaining, and feeling underappreciated. True/False
4. People with passive-aggressive behavior should be hospitalized. True/False
5. When dealing with passive aggressive people the best reply is *whatever*. True/False
6. Getting angry at passive aggressive people, is the best advice. True/False
7. Japanese culture may be wrongly interpreted as passive aggressive behavior. True/False
8. People can stop other people from being passive aggressive. True/False

Vocabulary Matching Activity
A. Match the words from the article on the left with the synonyms or definitions on the right.
1. assertive
2. antagonism
3. sullen
4. cynical
5. exhibit
6. whatever
7. dismissive
8. contempt
9. Plan B
10. harmonious

a) gloomy
b) distrustful
c) display
d) hostility
e) alternative arrangement
f) disrespect
g) agreeable
h) self-confident
i) doesn't really matter
j) indifferent

B. Now, choose four of the words on the left side from the above vocabulary exercise and write four sentences below using each of those words in a sentence.
a) _____
b) _____
c) _____
d) _____

Advice
Underline which advice you think is best for dealing with passive aggressive behavior or add your own in the bottom. Then discuss with your classmates your answers.
- State your confusion about the mixed messages they are sending
- Ask questions to show their inconsistencies.
- Pay more attention to what they do than what they say.
- Don't give them a chance to solve the problem.
- Respond by being silent and not speaking to them for a while.
- Hold them accountable for their promises not their results.
- Be defensive and argue with any criticism they may have.
- Your own advice _____

Classroom Discussion Questions
Write four questions for class discussion based on the article. Next, ask your classmates your questions and make sure they give reasons.
a) _____
b) _____
c) _____
d) _____

Please discuss the questions below with your classmates. Give detailed answers.
1. What is good behavior ? What is bad behavior?
2. Is there any behavior that you would not find acceptable?
3. Why do you think that assertive training is often taught in business?
4. How would you deal with a passive-aggressive co-worker?
5. How would you deal with a passive-aggressive supervisor?

The Fourth Type Lesson Notes

_____
_____
_____
_____
_____
_____
_____
_____
_____
_____
_____

Today's Vocabulary

Words	Synonym	Antonym	Definition

Collocations/Phrases	Definition

What did I learn today?
_____
_____
_____

What do I need to improve?
_____
_____
_____

My homework for next class
_____
_____
_____

I Wear My Heart upon My Sleeve

Warm Up

Shakespeare Reading Assignment
Before reading the article find a synopsis of Othello

Shakespeare Quotes Activity
With a partner, paraphrase the following quotes from William Shakespeare.

A fool thinks himself to be wise, but a wise man knows himself to be a fool.
As You Like It
_____

Some are born great, some achieve greatness, and some have greatness thrust upon them.
Twelfth Night
_____

The evil that men do lives after them; the good is oft interred with their bones.
Julius Caesar
_____

The course of true love never did run smooth.
A Midsummer Night's Dream
_____

Classroom Discussion Questions
1. What makes a great villain?
2. Can you give an example of a great villain?

Heroes vs. Villains Matching
Match the fictional hero with his villain

1. Batman
2. Superman
3. Othello
4. Lupin III
5. Thor
6. Luke Skywalker
7. Clarice Starling
8. Van Helsing
9. James Bond
10. Nobita

a) Auric Goldfinger
b) Dracula
c) Hannibal Lector
d) Loki
e) Darth Vader
f) Gian
g) Inspector Zenigata
h) Joker
i) Lex Luthor
j) Iago

Villain Looks Description
Using your imagination, describe what a typical villain looks like

Sex _____ Age _____ Height _____
Build _____ Clothing _____
Hair Color_____ Hair Style _____
Eyes _____ Facial Features _____
Distinguishing Features _____
_____

Other Comments _____
_____
_____

I Wear My Heart upon My Sleeve

The often-quoted line, "I wear my heart upon my sleeve," comes from one of Shakespeare's greatest villains, Iago in *Othello*. He professes to everyone that anyone can easily see his emotions, but in truth, he hides his real feelings, so that people do not suspect his cunning and evil plans to destroy Othello.

What does this have to do with business? For instance at a meeting, is everyone there to make sure that the meeting objectives are met? Are there other factors that might hinder a meeting from succeeding?

In meetings, one can often observe people's motivations that are more obvious. People will often state that their actions and plans are to see the company, section, or organization succeed. Everyone should share this pronounced goal and claim this rationale as their primary guide for all decisions. However, if one looks closer, you can observe more personal motivational factors. The motivation could want to be loved, to be wealthy, to be safe, and to be respected and so on. People's motivations are varied and often many people are unaware of what motivates them.

However, a few people are well aware of what motivates them and try to keep it hidden. Some of these individuals keep this driving force private and this will be their primary guide in all decisions. This behavior is called "having a hidden agenda." The American Heritage Dictionary says that a hidden agenda is "an undisclosed plan, especially one with an ulterior motive." An ulterior motive is a motive that is different from the stated motive or reason.

The hidden agenda goal can be someone wanting to achieve a position of power or prestige at the expense of others. Perhaps the person desires to dominate or control other people. In addition, they may enjoy putting other people down or make other people feel bad about themselves. Luckily, Iago types are rare, but people can cause trouble because of envy and a previous lack of recognition.

If you are wondering why your meetings are not getting the results you want, yet you are managing the meetings well then maybe you are facing someone with a hidden agenda. Signs of hidden agenda existing could be a proposal pushed though with little analysis and discussion. Was the extent of a problem exaggerated? Did you feel confused and angry about the results after the meeting?

What to do when you think someone has a hidden agenda? First, observe what they say and how they say it and then analyze it. What was their line of reasoning? Does it make sense? Is it logical? A good rule is when a proposal is made and you are uncertain about its purpose then postpone. Wait until you and other members have had a chance to think it over. If your intuition feels that something is wrong, then listen to your intuition and show you have some reservations and ask for time.

When you feel that something is going awry and someone is secretly sabotaging the meeting, then you have to keep your cool. Not getting angry will maintain your credibility and denies a saboteur the satisfaction of seeing you upset. Also, do not point the finger and lay blame on the backstabber, as this will make you look childish and petty. The saboteur does not like his actions to be easily seen by everyone so speak up and ask questions in a way that people have to explain their actions. It requires patience and determination, but it is an important step to regaining control of the meeting.

Finally repeat the objective by restating the reason for the meeting, the reason for your opinion and that the focus is to keep the meeting productive. Hopefully, all of this advice will help if you have to deal with your own Iago.

© David Baird

I Wear My Heart upon My Sleeve Activity Sheet

Reading Comprehension Quiz

Circle your answers based on the reading

1. According to the article, people's personal motivational factors will not be ...
    a) to be loved.
    b) to be hate.
    c) to be rich.
    d) to be secure.
2. "I wear my heart upon my sleeve," means
    a) People can easily see my emotions
    b) I am shy and reserved
    c) I often lie
    d) My arm is bleeding
3. Ulterior means:
    a) Transparent
    b) Super
    c) Obvious
    d) Hidden
4. Who is Iago?
    a) A parrot
    b) The villain in Othello
    c) Frankenstein's assistant
    d) The hero in Othello
5. In the article, the writer stated, a person with a hidden agenda may want to ...
    a) Help promote people
    b) Obtain power
    c) See their friends do well
    d) Rule the planet
6. When you think a hidden agenda may exist, the article advises you to ...
    a) observe and do not make quick decisions.
    b) observe and make quick decisions.
    c) confront the person whose hidden agendas are causing you problems.
    d) ignore the hidden agenda.

Vocabulary Matching Activity

A. Match the words on the left with the words on the right that have a similar meaning.

1. villain
2. professes
3. hinder
4. rationale
5. dominate
6. intuition
7. sabotaging
8. petty
9. backstabber
10. keep your cool

a) basis
b) feeling
c) bad guy
d) direct
e) don't get excited
f) admits
g) secretly damaging
h) unfair attacker
i) delay
j) small-minded

B. Now, choose five words on the left side from the above vocabulary exercise and write five sentences below using each of those words in a sentence.

a) _____
b) _____
c) _____
d) _____
e) _____

Classroom Discussions Questions

Please discuss the questions below with your classmates. Make sure to ask follow up questions. Give detailed answers.

1) How do you deal with deceitful people?
2) Which is worse, the evil we can see or the evil that is hidden?
3) Do people play a lot of politics in your company?
4) Is having a hidden agenda a good thing or bad thing?
5) Does your company's management generally condone people who do things behind other people's backs?
6) Do your department's meetings get the results you want? Why or why not?
7) Do you think most foreigners would find *nemawashi* deceitful and frustrating? Why?

Write discussion questions for class discussions based on the topic in the article. Next, ask your classmates your questions and make sure they give reasons.

a) _____
b) _____
c) _____

I Wear My Heart upon My Sleeve Lesson Notes

_____
_____
_____
_____
_____
_____
_____
_____
_____
_____
_____

Today's Vocabulary

Words	Synonym	Antonym	Definition

Collocations/Phrases	Definition

What did I learn today?
_____
_____
_____

What do I need to improve?
_____
_____
_____
_____

My homework for next class
_____
_____
_____

© David Baird

I'm Shy

Warm Up

International Greetings Matching Activity
Match the language with how to say hello in that language
1. French
2. German
3. Korean
4. Thai
5. Hebrew
6. Russian
7. Chinese
8. Arabic
9. Spanish
10. Hawaiian

a) Guten Tag
b) Ahn Nyeong
c) Marhabah
d) Ni Hao
e) Aloha
f) ¡Hola
g) Bonjour
h) Sawadee-krap (man) Sawadee-ka (woman)
i) Shalom
j) Privet

Good Ice Breaker/Bad Ice Breaker Activity
Write after each phrase whether the phrases you think are good icebreakers or bad icebreakers.

1. Are you finished with your paper?
2. Is this the way to _____?
3. You look fit. Do you play any sports?
4. Are you married?
5. How do you know the host?
6. Would you like to be my friend?
7. You look like you're having a great day
8. Guess what? It's your lucky day. Out of all the people here, I picked you to talk to.
9. What do you do?
10. You look very familiar, have we met before?
11. Wow! I had no idea they made women's shoes that big!
12. Have you been with the company long?
13. So, who are you going to vote for?
14. Don't you agree that the central bank's policy is going to cause a recession?
15. It looks like rain. Do you know what the forecast is today?
16. That was interesting. What did you think of the speaker?

Socializing Survey
Answer the survey. Then discuss your answers with a classmate.

1. Do you enjoy meeting people for the first time?   Yes/No
2. Are you nervous when meeting a Japanese person for the first time?   Yes/No
3. Are you nervous when meeting a foreigner for the first time?   Yes/No
4. Do you think you make a good first impression?   Yes/No
5. Who has recently made a good first impression with you?
   _____
6. Would you consider your self to be an extrovert (outgoing and friendly) or an introvert (quiet and shy)?
7. Is making small talk an easy thing for you?   Yes/No
8. How do you usually break the ice? (start a conversation)?
   _____
9. What do you like to talk about
   at work _____ at a party _____
   at home _____ with strangers _____
10. What do you **not** like to talk about with co-workers or strangers?
    _____

I'm Shy

If an English teacher in Japan were to receive ¥100 for every time they heard their students say, "I'm shy," most of the teachers would be able to retire to Hawaii by the age of 55. However, there cannot be so many shy Japanese, for then there would be no one to sell anything; Japan would be a silent country with few TV shows; and no sales people. Most of all there would probably be a lot less Japanese as men and women would be afraid to talk to each other.

What Japanese are really trying to say instead is, "I'm not confident when meeting strangers, especially in English." Well Japanese can join the club as there are people all over the world who feel the same. There are countless books and websites in multiple languages that counsel people on how to overcome their fear of meeting new people.

So how can someone be more confident when meeting strangers and not be crippled by shyness. The first step is to change your attitude to be outward looking and not focus on yourself. Pretend that you are an outgoing friendly person and then after some practice and times you will start to believe it.

To help become surer of yourself, change your body language by standing in a confident manner for two minutes a day. Research shows that using powerful body language can actually change a person's hormones and behavior so to command attention you just have to practice standing confidently. When confident body language becomes second nature then behavior will change, which will lead to more positive social interactions.

The next thing is to prepare a strategy to break the ice. Try by making a comment when you are sharing a similar experience, such as at a seminar, standing in line or waiting for a meeting to start. Break the ice by making a comment, or statement, often followed by a question. Sample lines could be; "*This conference is really crowded. Is it like this every year?*" or "*Wow, it's hot in here, I wonder if the air conditioner is on?*"

After you have gotten a response, then ask a follow up question. The secret to opening a conversation with a stranger is not what you say but rather what you ask. The best topic is to get the other person talking about him or herself. You have to realize the other person is also feeling uncomfortable, more than likely feels the same way as you so he or she will appreciate a person trying to initiate a conversation.

After initiating the conversation, you have to move on to the small talk. To make great small talk, you should keep things light, fun, and upbeat. When making small talk, you should avoid talking about anything too negative, too personal or the other person will be put off.

However, what small talk subject is ideal? Finding the right topic is often a dilemma for many. Now some self-help authors may suggest the weather, a complement, work or your surroundings. Be prepared by having a few stock questions that you can use with different people in a variety of situations. Think of standard questions about the host or the organization hosting the event such as how do you know the host, is this your first time at this event, etc.

Do not let your attention wander or start glancing at your smart phone. Either one of these things shows you are not interested. Make your conversational partner feel as if they are the most important person on the planet so keep focused on him or her. Also, listen to things that the person says so you can guide the conversation to a livelier area. The person may make a small comment that is tangential to your question or topic, so keep your ears open and see if something your new acquaintance says can trigger a new line of conversation.

Meeting new people and having to make small talk is not everyone's favorite activity, but if you make a conscious effort to improve and use some of the tips provided, you might find yourself enjoying life a lot more.

© David Baird

I'm Shy Activity Sheet

True and False Quiz

Based on the reading, circle whether the statements are true or false.

1. Most English teachers can retire early to Hawaii because they are paid so well. — True/False
2. Japanese are extremely shy people. — True/False
3. To stop being afraid of meeting new people, people can get advice from websites and books. — True/False
4. The first step to being more confident is to change your outlook. — True/False
5. Posing in a confident manner for two minutes a day will make you more confident. — True/False
6. Most people are comfortable with meeting strangers. — True/False
7. Great small talk should be light, fun, and gossipy. — True/False
8. Good small topics are the weather, a complement, work or money. — True/False
9. Playing with your smart phone is now socially acceptable. — True/False
10. Being good at small talk will make your life more enjoyable. — True/False

Vocabulary Matching Activity

A. Match the words from the reading on the left with similar meaning words on the right

1. counsel
2. crippled
3. small talk
4. initiating
5. acquaintance
6. upbeat
7. second nature
8. stock
9. tangential
10. trigger
11. conscious

a) generating
b) starting
c) cheerful
d) advise
e) conventional
f) mindful
g) contact
h) chit-chat
i) impaired
j) habit pattern
k) unrelated

B. Now, choose five of the words from the above vocabulary exercise and write five sentences below using each of those words in a sentence.
   Example: *I would counsel you to reconsider your choice.*
   a) _____
   b) _____
   c) _____
   d) _____
   e) _____

Classroom Discussion Questions

Please discuss the questions below with your classmates. Give detailed answers and ask follow up questions when necessary.

1. Are Japanese people truly shy?
2. Can a shy person become fluent in a second language?
3. What advice would you give someone to overcome his or her shyness?
4. What is your strategy when meeting someone new?
5. What is your strategy when in a room with people you do not know?
6. What is the best opening line you have ever heard to break the ice?
7. What do you like to talk about when chatting with friends?
8. Are you generally upbeat?

Write discussion questions for class discussions based on the topic in the article.
   a) _____
   b) _____
   c) _____
   d) _____
   e) _____

I'm Shy Lesson Notes

_____
_____
_____
_____
_____
_____
_____
_____
_____
_____
_____

Today's Vocabulary

Words	Synonym	Antonym	Definition

Collocations/Phrases	Definition

What did I learn today?
_____
_____
_____

What do I need to improve?
_____
_____
_____

My homework for next class
_____
_____
_____

© David Baird

Being Great

Warm Up

Leadership Qualities

With a partner, choose seven qualities from the two columns on the right on what you believe are qualities that a leader needs to be successful.

1. _____
2. _____
3. _____
4. _____
5. _____
6. _____
7. _____

a) Ability to motivate
b) Ambitious
c) Business-savvy
d) Commitment
e) Strong communication skills
f) Creativity
g) Cunning
h) Decisiveness
i) High emotional intelligence
j) Hard working
k) Honesty
l) Humility
m) Image conscience
n) Industry knowledge
o) Integrity
p) Intelligence
q) Intractableness
r) Micro manager
s) Patience
t) Positive attitude
u) Recognize followers strengths
v) Risk-taking
w) Role model
x) Ruthlessness
y) Self-awareness
z) Worthy of respect

Choose Your Boss

Below are some famous people. Which one of these men would you like to be your boss? Write your reasons below. (You answer should be 150 words or more)

The Best Boss would be ...

_____

Not to be copy or reproduced in any form unless granted permission

Being Great

What makes a great leader? Is it something that a person is born to be or do people achieve greatness or is it something that happens due to circumstances? The answer to this centuries old question is as varied as the people seeking explanations.

Now business schools are studying this puzzle as leading a large organization is not easy. A CEO of an established company must keep moving the company forward if it wants to survive. To successfully shift an organization in any direction requires considerable effort and skill as an organization is a bulky and nearly inert mass. A CEO will face people who are accustomed to doing and thinking in a certain way so often these stakeholders will resist change.

Jim Collins, renowned consultant and teacher has studied successful and unsuccessful companies for over 20 years and has obtained a few illuminating insights on what makes a successful CEO. One surprising result from his research that went against conventional wisdom is that most successful leaders came from inside a company and they were not outside saviors who arrived with much fanfare.

Collins points out that the first thing a successful CEO does is to gather a strong team around him. The most important asset is to have the right people around the CEO. Moreover, the CEO needs dissenting and contrasting viewpoints to keep hubris in check so he should not surround himself with sycophants and yes-men.

After gathering a team, then the executive should decide, what the company is and how do its customer view the company and its products. The chief will also need to assess the organization's strengths and weaknesses along with its corporate culture. After that, the executive team can formulate a strategy. These steps make perfect sense, as a company cannot execute a strategy unless there are first skilled people in place.

Other ways to identify what makes a great leader is looking at the habits of very bad leaders and, unfortunately, there are many examples. One example of terrible leadership is a CEO, who sees the company as an extension of themselves, as his personal empire. They often enjoy the spotlight too much. A CEO believing he is god so he and his organization can do no wrong sometimes possesses this outlook. They overlook or underestimate the difficulty of achieving goals

This behavior can lead to two different destructive results. One is the abuse of power where the company is seen as a personal bank accountant by senior management. This conduct led to the downfall of the Medici bank in 1494 to the near collapse of Tyco in 2002. The other possible result is going into businesses that the company should not even consider such as Samsung venturing into the car business.

There are other bad habits such as rashly deciding without grasping the ramifications; eliminating dissent by pushing out independent thinking lieutenants; clinging to old concepts and methods or quickly changing plans to follow the newest fad.

One last bad habit, which even the best CEO can succumb to, is not perceiving when to leave. A CEO should understand that he or she must have an exit strategy and prepare their succession, as the company needs another great leader not a middling one. As Paul Thompson, an Australian CEO who did retire said, "It is far too easy for a founding CEO to stay too long. It is healthier for an organization for the founder to leave too early than stay too late."

Looking at good and bad executives, one quality sticks out as defining an outstanding leader has first and foremost one goal, to make his or her company the best. He or she understands that the company may suffer severe setbacks, but the CEO believes it will bounce back. The tactics and the strategy will probably need to be adapted, big operations may have to be shut down and failed business ideas shelved, but the pursuit of excellence never stops for him or her.

© David Baird

Being Great Activity Sheet

True or False Quiz

Based on the reading, circle whether the statements are true or false.

1. Philosophers, military leaders, writers and business schools examine leadership. — True/False
2. A CEO wanting to make changes will be challenged by employees resistant to change. — True/False
3. Hiring a new president from outside is what most companies should do. — True/False
4. A new leader should decide on a strategy first and build a team second. — True/False
5. A CEO should have people around him who agree with him/her 100% of the time. — True/False
6. Samsung manufacturing cars was a very good business idea. — True/False
7. A bad sign of a leader is one who enjoys the spotlight too much. — True/False
8. Outstanding CEOs should stay as long as possible for they are the only ones who know how to keep the company profitable. — True/False
9. A great leader never gives up. — True/False

Vocabulary Matching Activity

A. Match the words from the article on the left with the synonyms or definitions on the right.

1. bulky
2. illuminating
3. fanfare
4. big ego
5. sycophants
6. hubris
7. venturing
8. abuse
9. ramifications
10. succumb
11. middling

a) exploitation
b) surrender
c) second-rate
d) flatterer
e) inflated self-importance
f) consequences
g) unwieldy
h) enlightening
i) investing
j) publicity
k) arrogance

B. Now, choose five of the words on the left column from the above vocabulary exercise and write five sentences below using each of those idioms in a sentence.

Example: He has such a *big ego*; I'm surprised he can get his head into the room.

a) _____
b) _____
c) _____
d) _____
e) _____

Classroom Discussion Questions

Please discuss the questions below with your classmates. Ask follow up questions and give detailed answers.

1. Who do you think is a great leader?
2. How would you evaluate leadership skills?
3. How would you rate your leadership skills?
4. What CEOs do you think have done a good job recently?
5. What CEOs do you think have done a poor job recently?
6. Which woman do you think would make a great CEO?
7. If you were organizing an executive team what type of people would you want?
8. What should a company do if the CEO sees the company as an extension of himself or herself or as his/her personal empire?
9. Which CEOs do you think have stayed too long?

Write discussion questions for class discussions based on the topic in the article.

a) _____
b) _____
c) _____
d) _____

Being Great Notes

_____
_____
_____
_____
_____
_____
_____
_____
_____
_____

Today's Vocabulary

Words	Synonym	Antonym	Definition

Collocations/Phrases	Definition

What did I learn today?
_____
_____
_____

What do I need to improve?
_____
_____
_____

My homework for next class
_____
_____
_____

© David Baird

Clothes Make the Man and Woman

Warm Up

Know Your Clothes

Group the following words into the proper sections below.

mules	jeans	tuxedo	gown	jersey	skirt
shawl	brassier	girdle ascot	tee-shirt	beret	sash
Stetson cloche sneakers		sandals	loafers	slacks	blouse
kilt	parka	watch cap	overalls	cardigan	chinos
capris	suspenders	sarong veil	culottes	belt vest	socks
fedora	watch	pantsuit	flats Hawaiian shirt		stockings
blazer	sweater	bowtie	trousers	pajamas	earrings
dress shirt	flip-flops	windbreaker	tank top	purse	hoodie

Men's Clothes	Women's Clothes	Unisexual Clothes	Accessories	Hats	Shoes

Fashion Quotes

With a classmate, paraphrase the following statements.

1. Fashion fades, only style remains the same.
   _____
   _____

2. Fashion is a language. Some know it, some learn it, some never will – like an instinct.
   _____
   _____

3. Fashion should be a form of escapism, and not a form of imprisonment.
   _____
   _____

4. Whoever said that money can't buy happiness, simply didn't know where to go shopping.
   _____
   _____

5. In order to be irreplaceable, one must always be different.
   _____
   _____

Dress Code

If you could decide the dress code for your company, what would be permissible?

For men
_____
_____
_____

For women
_____
_____
_____
_____

Clothes Make the Man and Woman

Noted American television reporter and commentator, Linda Ellerbee once stated, "If men can run the world, why can't they stop wearing neckties? How intelligent is it to start the day by tying a little noose around your neck?" This viewpoint brought about the retort that women cannot be too smart either as they wear high heels. What both men and women may agree on is that they often wear uncomfortable clothes to look good.

According to Virgin owner, Richard Branson the necktie is an odd accessory, as it serves no useful purpose. He and other professionals see the tie as constricting and ugly. A new argument against ties has been raised that neckties are a health hazard. The British Medical Association now tells doctors to stop wearing ties as they accumulate all types of bacteria. Unluckily for men who are not doctors, wearing a necktie is still compulsory in many companies' dress codes.

Luckily, for men, the tie is disappearing from dress codes for a variety of reasons. The first reason is the influence of the Information Technology industry. The IT industry has its roots in the counter-culture of California where the necktie was seen as a repressive symbol of authority that stifled self-expression. Their attitude has influenced other industries to change their dress codes so now business casual is becoming the norm, which consists of nice chinos, loafers and a short-sleeved shirt.

In Japan, the Cool Biz program instituted by former Prime Minister Junichiro Koizumi to help lower energy consumption has made the once strongly conservative Japanese slowly adopt a more relaxed dress code. However, some old school holdouts in Japanese business still staunchly embrace wearing a suit and tie, no matter the occasion or weather. Even so, the tie is slowly losing its place as a badge of professionalism.

Fortunately, for women, they do not have to wear neckties but they have other fashion dilemmas to contend with. Women's business attire is generally patterned after male business attire—a suit consisting of a jacket with matching skirt or slacks, plus a blouse. As women have a greater variety of clothes to wear, women have more leeway on what is an acceptable form of business attire. However, because of the variety, in many businesses the dress codes for women go into more detail on what clothes are permissible.

In Japan and many Asian countries, many offices still require women to wear a uniform while their male counterparts do not. Feminists have made the case that uniforms marginalize women. The argument is women in uniform are not treated as equals by their male counterparts and supervisors, so they will never be considered as candidates for promotion nor have their opinions taken seriously.

Still some women are fans of work uniforms. For uniform supporters, uniforms allow them to save money, as they do not have to spend money to buy clothes for work. Additionally while the uniform may not be attractive, they are often more durable and cost less to clean. Even with these benefits, the uniform is losing its popularity, as companies do not want to bear the cost nor are many young people willing to wear it as uniforms stifle their individuality.

The decline in uniforms and the move to more casual attire shows that attitudes toward clothing are evolving. Where this evolution will lead to, no one really knows. Perhaps with global warning, business attire in 2050 will be sandals, cargo shorts and Hawaiian shirts for men and wedges, tank tops and Capri pants for women.

© David Baird

Clothes Make the Man or Woman Activity Sheet

True or False Quiz
Based on the reading, circle whether the statements are true or false
1. Linda Ellerbee thought men were clever because they wear ties. — True/False
2. Richard Branson thinks the necktie is an odd accessory, as it serves no useful purpose. — True/False
3. The British Medical Association now recommends doctors to wear ties so the ties can collect germs. — True/False
4. The IT Industry has influenced people to wear more casual attire. — True/False
5. The Cool Biz program was started by Prime Minister Koizumi. — True/False
6. The standard attire for businesswomen is a dark suit. — True/False
7. Feminists believe that uniforms elevate women. — True/False
8. Uniforms help women save money, as they do not need money for work clothes. — True/False
9. Global warming will make Hawaiian shirts the standard business attire. — True/False

Vocabulary Matching Activity
A. Match the words from the article on the left with the synonyms or definitions on the right.

1. retort
2. constricting
3. repressive
4. stifled
5. staunchly
6. old school
7. badge
8. leeway
9. permissible
10. marginalize
11. durable
12. evolving

a) steadfastly
b) suppressive
c) long-lasting
d) allowable
e) undervalue
f) held back
g) quip
h) confining
i) changing
j) symbol
k) flexibility
l) conservative

B. Now, choose six of the words on the left column from the above vocabulary exercise and write six sentences below using each of those words in a sentence.
a) ___
b) ___
c) ___
d) ___
e) ___
f) ___

Classroom Discussion Questions
Please discuss the questions below with your classmates. Give detailed answers
1. Are you a big fan of ties? What are the pros and cons of ties?
2. Are women foolish to wear high heels? What are the pros and cons of high heels?
3. Are you concerned about clothes?
4. What type of clothes would you like to wear to work?
5. How would your business associates judge you if you wore more casual clothes?
6. What is your company's dress code?
7. Do you think you are fashionable? Why?
8. How would you describe your fashion sense?
9. What kind of clothes do you like best?
10. When it comes to clothes, whose clothes are more comfortable men or women?

Write additional questions for class discussion based on the article's theme.
a) ___
b) ___
c) ___
d) ___

Clothes Make the Man or Woman Notes

_____
_____
_____
_____
_____
_____
_____
_____
_____
_____
_____

Today's Vocabulary

Words	Synonym	Antonym	Definition

Collocations/Phrases	Definition

What did I learn today?
_____
_____
_____

What do I need to improve?
_____
_____
_____

My homework for next class
_____
_____
_____

People Articles Vocabulary Review

Sentence Scramble
Unscramble the words and put them in the correct order to make a proper sentence.

1. on/firms/Some/counsel/the/elevator/their/staff/not/to/talk/business

2. accidently/reveal/The/company/firms/may/the/staff/believe/secrets.

3. often/it/can/admired/disastrous/yet/consequences/trigger/Hubris/is/

4. reliability/and/The/IT/ industry/durability/ seldom/discusses/

5. he/tired/of/the/his/was/rat/Because/getting/chicken/quit/job/feed/race/and/Takahiro/

6. are/the/allow/some/circumstances/we/leeway/Given/going/to/?

7. His/fed/by/big/sycophants/his/ego/

8. was/and/at/best/pony/middling/their/dog/show/It

9. ramifications/of/date/thinking/their/rarely/see/of/out/Dinosaurs/the

10. funds/Many/people/have/contempt/for/vulture/

11. a/constricting/tie/can/be/Wearing

12. do/has/a/hidden/you/do/when/someone/What/agenda?

Word Form Choice
Choose the correct form of the word in the sentences below.

1. He has *repressed/repressing/repressive/repression* all opposition to his plans.
2. Considerable *scientific/science* research is slowly revealing the truth of how man *evolution/evolving/evolved*.
3. Nothing *venturing/ventured*, nothing gained.
4. When you buy things in *bulky/bulk* you often get a discount.
5. His *initiation/initiative/initiated/initiating* was admired by his bosses, but not by his co-workers.
6. The *losts/losses* by the Australian subsidiary were *crippling/crippled* to the company.
7. The heat today is *stifled/stifling*.
8. His *abusive/abuse/abusing/abused* behavior has made his section the worst one in the company.
9. He is not a *rational/rationale/rationalized* human being.
10. His influence weakened by his *cynic/cynical/cynicism* and his prickly nature.

People Articles Vocabulary Review

Dialogue Activity
In each of the dialogues below put the words in the box into the appropriate blanks below.

Dialogue 1

| night owl | doghouse | delaying | illuminating |
| business savvy | commitment | creativity | ambition |

A: Oh man I am ever in the _____!
B: What did you do wrong now?
A: You know I'm a _____. Well I was up until 4, surfing the Net, so I slept in and came late to a very important kick off meeting for a really big project.
B: How late were you?
A: I was about 30 minutes late. After the meeting, I was pulled into a private meeting with my boss and another manager.
B: What happened then?
A: My boss told me that I was not showing enough_____ and _____ and I lacked a professional attitude. It was all for show so people could think he is a tough guy. I mean the week before he was telling me how I am the heart and soul of the team.
B: You seem a little angry at about this.
A: I didn't mind being criticized because I was in the wrong, but there was no need for the other manager to be there. And I didn't like the language he used.
B: So what are you going to do?
A: Well, it was an _____ conversation, but as for now I am going to be my usual hard working self, using my _____ and _____ to make this project a success.
B: That's it?
A: No, I am _____ doing anything now, but I plan to quit by the end of the year.

Dialogue 2

snakes	big ego	contempt	fanfare
patience	Plan B	sycophants	antagonistic
rationale	ramifications	sabotage	positive attitude

A: Hi Kaz, how's work going?
B: Not too good. I'm leading a new project and it's not going so well.
A: Really? What's the problem?
B: You heard about our purchase of Shomani?
A: Yeah. That was announced with a lot of _____ two months ago.
B: Well, I am in charge of the post-acquisition integration and it's trying my _____. The mangers at Shomani are all bunch of _____ who are trying to _____ our integration efforts. They don't see the _____ behind our plans.
A: Well Kaz, I think you need to keep your cool.
B: Easy to say, but you have never had to deal with Mori-san, my counterpart. The guy has a _____ and is surrounded by _____. He is blocking all our plans.
A: Why do you think he is doing that?
B: My guess is that he is afraid of losing his status, perhaps even his job, so he has become _____ towards all our plans. His remarks at the last meeting displayed deep _____, so no one treats us with respect.
A: Do you have a _____?
B: Yeah, and it's not pretty. I am going to have a meeting with everyone and tell them we need them to have a more _____ and be more receptive or else.
A: What is the "or else?"
B: We'll offer them buyouts or transfer them to branch offices where they'll stay forever.
A: That's very harsh.
B: It may be but they need to see that their actions have _____.
A: Well good luck, I hope it all works out.

People Articles Review

What Do You Think?

Give written answers to the following questions. Give a full explanation to each of your answers.

1. What makes a great leader?

2. How would you describe your taste in clothes?

3. What advice would give to someone who wants to be more sociable?

4. How would you describe *nemawashi* to foreigners?

5. Who do you think is crying wolf?

6. Do you need assertive training?

What Have You Learned So Far?

Write your thoughts on what the most interesting, most surprising, most controversial topic that you have discussed from the People Section.

My Boss Has No Clothes

Warm Up

Classroom Discussion Questions
1. What was your favorite fairy tale growing up? Why?
2. Are fairy tales a good tool to teach morals?

Parables
Can you explain the moral lesson from the following Aesop Tales?

The Tortoise and the Hare
_____
_____

The Boy Who Cried Wolf
_____
_____

The Grasshopper and the Ants
_____
_____

Phrase Classification
Classify each of the phrases for disagreement below as polite, rude or informal. Write **P** after the polite phrases, **r** after the rude phrases and **i** after the informal phrases.

Are you nuts?
I beg to differ.
I'm afraid I can't possibly support that
You're sadly mistaken.
I have to disagree about this
What about looking at it a different way?
Will that make everyone satisfied?
Not necessarily
Can we look at an alternative?
It makes me want to puke!

I can't go along with that.
You're kidding, right?
You're talking rubbish.
I'm not so sure.
I don't think so.
Can we look outside the box?
Do you really think so?
I find it difficult to support that
That's out of the question
Is that a good idea?

Disagreement Role Plays
Read your assigned roles and then role-play these disagreement situations in pairs. Try to reach a positive outcome.

Role Play 1
Student A: *Sales Team Leader*
You want to tell the boss that he is giving the team too much paperwork that is not allowing them enough time to do their job – selling!

Student B: *Sales Manager*
The head of one of the sales teams wants to talk to you about new administration requirements

Role Play 2
Student B: *IT Manager*
You are against the new changes in the company dress code, making all the IT staff wear suits and ties. Most of the staff has stated they will quit.

Student A: *Chief Information Officer*
You are the newly appointed CIO and you have instituted a new dress policy in where all male employees must wear suit and ties.

My Boss Has No Clothes

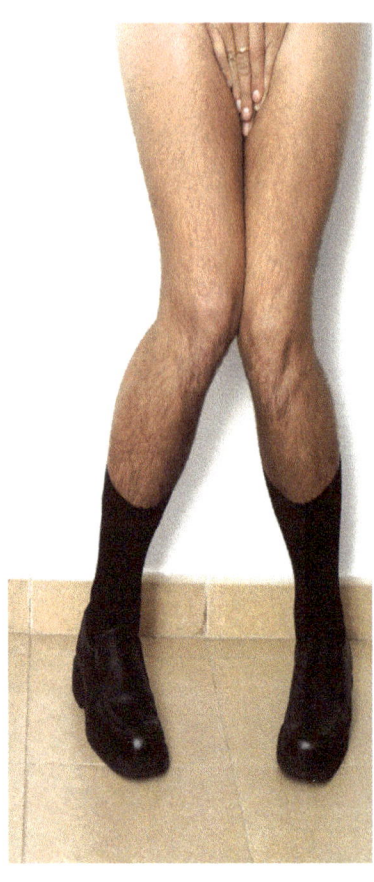

In 1837, Hans Christian Anderson wrote "*The Emperor's New Clothes.*" This well-known tale is about a vain Emperor who is only concerned about wearing the finest garments, hires two swindlers posing as tailors who promise him the finest suit of clothes. They promise that the clothes will be invisible to anyone who is unfit for his position or "hopelessly stupid."

Consequently, when the conmen dress the Emperor with his non-existent suit everyone pretends to see the suit. It is only when the Emperor is parading naked down the street that a child loudly exclaims the obvious, "The Emperor has no clothes." From that point the rest of the citizens join in and start repeating, "The Emperor has no clothes." Now in the story, the Emperor just continues walking down the street feeling embarrassed but still acts as if nothing happens. Additionally, the child is not punished.

The story has become one of Anderson's most famous one and the expression, "The Emperor has no clothes," is now a common saying to describe leaders that are oblivious to their own problems. However, it is perhaps a little unwise to tell your boss that he or she has no clothes as dissent and disagreement are seldom tolerated in most corporations.

So what do you do when you want to or need to disagree with your boss? Stating you learned a different method at university is not the way to win over your manager. As well, often telling him or her that you did it another way at your previous company, branch or section is usually not a persuasive technique, nor is bluntly crying out that they are wrong a good idea.

Many experts advise to disagree politely and diplomatically when dealing with supervisors and upper management. Senior management does not want to hear about all the company problems and screw-ups, instead present the news to executive management in a way they want to hear it.

The first pointer on disagreeing is choose what to disagree about, remember that wanting to be right all the time is not important and is not the way to win friends and supporters. Wanting to be always right will label you as a know-it-all, quarrelsome and categorized as the difficult person to work with and to be avoided. Choose fights that you can win and are worth winning.

The next step is when and where to disagree. If possible, raise your objections in private and when the boss has free time. Additionally you have to read your manager's signals to see if he or she is receptive at that moment to hear differing opinions.

How to disagree with your boss is probably the key fundamental. Before disagreeing, find out what makes the boss tick and feel out how he or she envisions the situation. How do you do that? Sample questions could be "Can you explain all the upsides of doing it this way?"; "What can we do to reduce any chance of our head office disagreeing with us?" By asking questions instead of disagreeing, you now become a team player

Then ask questions designed to help the manager see what you want them to consider such as "Shouldn't we consider doing it this way?" or "In this situation, would ABC have any merit as an approach?" These kinds of questions may open up your boss to consider other possibilities. If you feel your boss is now receptive, then offer a plan. However, offer the plan as a hypothetical and ask for your manager's analysis and input. You have moved your disagreement from a confrontational situation to a non-confrontational teaching moment.

By using tact, politeness and patience, you can get the same results without losing your integrity. It takes time and self-control but it is in your best interests. Building a healthy relationship with your superiors will allow you initiate and execute plans more smoothly.

© David Baird

My Boss Has No Clothes Activity Sheet

True and False Quiz
Based on the reading, circle whether the statements are true or false.

1. Hans Christian Anderson penned the story "The Emperor's Old Clothes." — True/False
2. "The Emperor has no clothes," is now a popular saying to describe leaders who are ignorant of their own problems. — True/False
3. Dissent and disagreement are promoted in most corporations. — True/False
4. Many bosses respect most business theories taught in universities. — True/False
5. Using your previous company as an example is a good technique to persuade your boss that you are right. — True/False
6. The first thing to decide when disagreeing is when and where to disagree. — True/False
7. Asking questions is a good way to make your supervisor consider alternatives. — True/False
8. Making problems hypothetical puts them into a non-confrontational setting. — True/False

Vocabulary Matching Activity

A. Match the words from the reading to synonyms on the left

1. garments
2. swindler
3. dissent
4. oblivious
5. tolerate
6. diplomatically
7. bluntly
8. quarrelsome
9. envisions
10. make someone tick
11. hypothetical

a) something that motivates someone
b) tactfully
c) accept
d) clothing
e) theoretical
f) frankly
g) con artist
h) opposition
i) contentious
j) heedless
k) pictures in his/her mind

B. Now, choose six of the words from the left column and write six sentences below using each of those words in a sentence.

a) _____
b) _____
c) _____
d) _____
e) _____
f) _____
g) _____

Classroom Discussion Questions

Write your discussion questions based on the article. Next, ask your classmates your questions and make sure they give reasons and in-depth explanations for their answers.

1. _____
2. _____
3. _____
4. _____
5. _____

Additional Questions for Discussion

Discuss the questions below with your classmates. Give your reasons.

1. Have you ever told someone that he or she has no clothes?
2. Have you ever wished to tell someone that he or she has no clothes?
3. What is your usual technique in disagreeing with people?
4. Have you ever tried to apply what you learnt or did in one organization to another organization? Was it successful?
5. Do you consider yourself a team player? Do other people consider you a team player?
6. Who was your best boss? Why was he/she your best boss?
7. If someone cannot get along with his or her boss, what advice would you give him or her?

My Boss Has No Clothes Lesson Notes

Today's Vocabulary

Words	Synonym	Antonym	Definition

Collocations/Phrases	Definition

What did I learn today?

What do I need to improve?

My homework for next class

© David Baird

It's Just Business, Nothing Personal

Warm Up

Classroom Discussion Questions
1. Have you ever quit a job? Why did you quit?
2. Why do most people quit companies?
3. What is a black company?
4. Do you think blank companies are increasing?

Motivation Ranking
Read the list below and choose six of the factors, which you think, keeps employees at companies. Then rank them from the most important factor to least important.

Bad economy	Job enrichment	Easy commute
Dislike change	Learning and development	Money and rewards
Charismatic CEO	Good fringe benefits	Guiding principles
Career advancement	Other employees and the team	
Section achievements and results	Organization success and results	
Contribute to society	Company's status with family and friends	
Have authority and responsibility		

Motivation
What motivates you?
_____
_____

What things can cause you to lose your motivation?
_____
_____

What things can cause other people to lose their motivation?
_____
_____

Evaluation Role Play Activity
With a classmate, role-play the following situations. Try to be constructive when in the manager role.

Situation 1
Student A: You are the manager of a five-person team, but one member seems to spend too much talking to the staff, but not working. His work is often late and not working at the level of your section's standards.
Student B: You are the member of a five-person team and your manager wants to speak to you about your performance. You joined the team last year and are still trying to understand what is required from you.

Situation 2
Student B: You are a sales manager and have just seen one of your salespeople give a horrible presentation to a potential client. The salesperson did not look at the audience, spoke too quietly and his information was incorrect.
Student A: You are a salesperson and your manager wants to speak to you about your last presentation, which was not very successful.

Vocabulary Activity
Guess the meanings of the following expressions after reading the article.

It's just business, nothing personal	_____
follow suit	_____
leave for greener pastures	_____
in the doldrums	_____
lifeblood	_____

It's Just Business, Nothing Personal

Before murdering someone in the movie The Godfather, the characters would occasionally state, "It's just business, nothing personal." When evaluating staff, this is good advice to keep in mind, as job performance assessments should be about business and not become personal. Evaluations are a time to motivate employees and make them want to stay, not to become too personal so staff will want to leave.

Why is retaining employees crucial? The first reason is the cost factor. The Employment Policy Foundation states it costs a company an average of $15,000 per employee when they leave. Other HR consultants estimate the cost as much as 1.5 times of the salary for a lost employee. The bottom line is that it is expensive and time consuming to replace employees.

The next issue is the talent issue. As more companies rely on knowledge workers, people possess unique, valuable skill sets, and deep domain knowledge, the need for them is increasing. Knowledge workers are now the lifeblood of many firms so retaining this pool of talent is vital for the long-term health and success of a business.

Another consequence of high turnover is it upsets operations. If the company does not have key positions manned then the company cannot implement its strategy. The result is a disruption of the firm's operations. It may also lead to structural paralysis as deeply embedded organizational knowledge and learning will be lost.

After that, if the turnover rate increases then it starts a domino effect as other employees follow suit. When someone sees a co-worker or friend leaving for greener pastures then the staff member might consider it time, to leave. This might also happen to customers as well who see the people they have relied and built a relationship leaving. It is not difficult to see why most managers readily agree that keeping the best employees ensures customer satisfaction, sales and happy co-workers.

In Japan, retaining staff was never a strong concern because of the lifetime employment system, but that system is slowly eroding. Additionally many industries have been in the doldrums so working for them is no longer financially attractive, intellectually challenging or status enhancing. As well, there has been a rise of "black companies" firms that are not concerned with staff welfare. Therefore, if a company sees employee retention as important, it might want to look at a few key areas.

So how is a company supposed to hold on to employees? The first thing a company should do is to look at the salary levels. An employer should offer wages at the industry average. Employee compensation could also include stock options or other financial awards for employees who achieve performance targets. Moreover, raises should be meaningful not paltry as a ¥2,000 monthly raise could be as discouraging as no raise.

While salary is important, it is not the key factor in hanging on to people. Surveys have shown that people leave will often leave companies for a better environment over money. A difficult strategy but a successful one is to create an environment that is challenging. Not challenging as in long hours with little breaks, but an environment that stimulates and engages the employees' minds and helps develops them. Engagement keeps employees.

Some HR consultants also suggest offering perks like the occasional free pizza or having casual Friday as it makes people feel at home, and relaxed. Other ideas for employee retention are having opportunities for career growth, and open communication lines between managers and staff. Of course, consistent feedback is also more helpful than evaluations.

Nevertheless, before implementing any evaluation program, the employer has to understand that business is about its personnel, so the company has to make its people its number one priority. No people, no business.

© David Baird

It's Just Business, Nothing Personal
Activity Sheet

True or False Quiz
Based on the reading, circle whether the statements are true or false.
1. Conducting evaluations properly is important to retain employees. — True/False
2. Keeping employees is important because rehiring is an expensive process. — True/False
3. High staff turnover helps company operations stay sharp. — True/False
4. Many workers are generally happy to see others go as it gives them a chance to be promoted. — True/False
5. Company loyalty is diminishing in Japanese businesses. — True/False
6. The only way to hold on to staff is to pay them large amounts of money. — True/False
7. Any raise is better than no raise. — True/False
8. Physically challenging jobs are the best way to keep employees. — True/False
9. Ideas to keep staff are recognition, professional development and open communication lines between supervisors and staff. — True/False

Vocabulary Matching Activities

A. Match the words from the article on the left with the synonyms or definitions on the right.

1. perks
2. domain knowledge
3. manned
4. disruption
5. paralysis
6. domino effect
7. embedded
8. eroding
9. paltry
10. engagement

a) deteriorating
b) chain reaction
c) commitment
d) inactivity
e) worthless
f) extras
g) disturbance
h) area of expertise
i) entrenched
j) staffed

B. Now, choose six of the words from the left column and write six sentences below using each of those words in a sentence. You may change the form of the words.
a) ___
b) ___
c) ___
d) ___
e) ___
f) ___

Classroom Discussion Questions
Write discussion questions based on the article. Next, ask your classmates your questions and make sure they give reasons.
1. ___
2. ___
3. ___
4. ___
5. ___

Additional Questions for Discussion
Discuss the questions below with your classmates. Give your reasons.
1. Is your company good at retaining employees?
2. What is the best way to evaluate employees?
3. Should companies get rid of performance review and rankings?
4. Do you feel you have been evaluated fairly in your career?
5. What is more important for you high salary but a stressful job or middling salary but an engaging job?
6. Why would setting up an engaging environment be difficult to create?
7. Which perk would you like your company to offer?
8. Have you ever witnessed a company that had high turnover? If yes, why did it happen?
9. If you were the CEO, what would be your company's HR policy?

It's Just Business, Nothing Personal Lesson Notes

Today's Vocabulary

Words	Synonym	Antonym	Definition

Collocations/Phrases	Definition

What did I learn today?

What do I need to improve?

My homework for next class

I'm so Tired, My Mind is on the Blink

Warm Up

Vacation and Work Survey

Circle either yes or no based upon your previous vacations.
1. I read work-related emails and text messages. Yes/No
2. I received work-related phone calls. Yes/No
3. I wanted access to a document on my home or work computer. Yes/No
4. I used up all my vacation time every year. Yes/No
5. I was asked to do work by my boss, client or colleague. Yes/No
6. My boss encouraged me to take time off. Yes/No
7. I worked during my vacations, but I was not happy Yes/No
8. I refused to do any work during my holidays. Yes/No
9. I did not think about work at all during my vacation Yes/No
10. I traveled on my vacation. Yes/No
11. I felt refreshed after my vacation Yes/No
12. My vacation was long enough Yes/No

Paraphrase Activity

Put the following quotations into your own words.
1. Fatigue makes cowards of us all.
   _____
   _____

2. A well-spent day brings happy sleep.
   _____
   _____

3. Man should forget his anger before he lies down to sleep.
   _____
   _____

4. Even nice things don't make you happy when you're tired.
   _____
   _____

5. After all, the best part of a holiday is perhaps not so much to be resting yourself, as to see all the other fellows busy working.
   _____
   _____
   _____

Sleep Phrases

Circle the word below each sentence that would go best in the sentence.
1. I _____ to go to sleep at 11 every night.
   try   effort   struggle   fight
2. Alcohol _____ me sleepy.
   causes   brings   makes   tries
3. Don't worry, the baby is _____ sleeping.
   fitfully completely   totally   soundly
4. I like to sleep _____ on Saturday.
   over   in   at   of
5. The meeting was so boring that I _____ to sleep.
   drifted off   dripped off   fell into   overtook

Vocabulary Finding Activity

Scan the article and find words that have a similar meaning to the words on the right.
1. madness   _____
2. increases _____
3. vital   _____
4. gathers   _____
5. restrict   _____
6. stupid   _____

I'm so Tired; My Mind is on the Blink

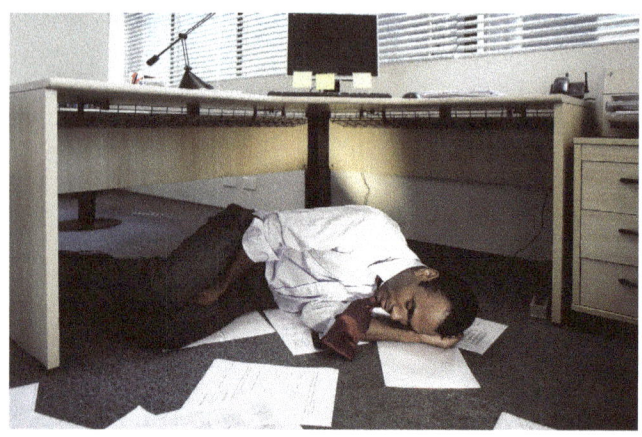

There are two things in this busy, fast-paced world that people often need, but never get, rest and sleep. As incessant noise and stress escalate, the need for people to disconnect from modern day insanity is becoming paramount. Sleep and vacations are not just important to physical and mental health but also for productivity.

In terms of health, lack of sleep can put people at risk of obesity, heart disease, high blood pressure, stroke and diabetes. As well, a recent study published in the prestigious magazine, *Science* has reinforced the importance of sleep to keep people's brains healthy. While sleeping, the brain is scrubbed clean of grey matter waste that accumulates each day and then the brain is reset so a person can start the day mentally and emotionally afresh. The cleansing time usually takes between six to eight hours.

If companies wanted their employees to be healthy, they should try to ensure that their employees are getting the proper amount of sleep. While some firms try to cap overtime hours, there are still many that do not. Numerous managers believe that working on little sleep is part of the job and a necessity for success.

Management's faulty outlook is not just dangerous for employees' health but also leads to lower productivity. Countless studies have pointed out that an insufficient amount of sleep can impair judgment, cause accidents and make people forgetful. Additionally little sleep weakens attention span, alertness, concentration, reasoning and problem solving, so overall sleepless employees results in dumb employees. If a company wants productive employees, it should limit overtime work and pay attention to job stress signals to ensure people are getting around 6.5 hours of sleep per night. As economic activity is becoming more knowledge based, sleep is especially even more important.

All of these findings make sense as people can observe from their own performance for the need for sleep, but what about its companion, rest. Sleep by itself is not enough, as people also need to relax and disconnect from work. Workers opting to forgo vacation time can lead to burnout, reduced productivity and diminished creativity. None of those results is beneficial for employees and a company.

However, managers and employees often think in the short term, so vacations are postponed until next year, as work is just too busy to get away and they fear falling behind in work. Additionally scheduling for vacation time in advance is too bothersome and time-consuming. Privately, employees are scared to be seen as weak or fear to be replaced if they do not give 110%. As well, they worry being viewed negatively with the vacation being used against them in the next performance review or promotion prospects.

So why should managers force their staff to take holidays? For the simple reason that they can get more productive and creative workers who may bring back from vacation some fresh insight. That justification might be difficult to measure, but there is other data that show the merits of staff taking vacations. Employees who take their two weeks off with pay get sick less and stay in the company longer. Vacations lower personnel costs over the long run.

Among developed economies, both Japanese and Americans are countries where workaholism is esteemed and are well known for not relaxing, taking holidays and having poor sleeping habits. However, for both of these countries' vaunted economic wealth, the workers seem not to receive even the simple reward of getting time off to enjoy life. Perhaps both countries should shift away from focusing on work to emphasizing living well. They might become happier.

© David Baird

I'm so Tired, My Mind is on the Blink Activity Sheet

True or False Quiz
Based on the reading, circle whether the statements are true or false.
1. Most people often get enough sleep and rest. — True/False
2. A lack of sleep makes people prone to getting fat, having heart attacks and strokes. — True/False
3. Our brains are cleaned of grey matter waste during the day so we can sleep peacefully at night. — True/False
4. Numerous supervisors think that very little sleep is required for employees to succeed. — True/False
5. Research shows that not enough sleep can weaken decision-making. — True/False
6. If a company limits employees' overtime then people should be more productive. — True/False
7. Workers often think that going on vacation will harm their chances for success. — True/False
8. Managers are recommended to push their staff to go on vacation. — True/False
9. Workaholism is admired in Japan but not in the USA. — True/False
10. Japanese and Americans are the happiest people in the world. — True/False

Vocabulary Match Activity
A. Match the words from the reading on the left with similar meaning words on the right.

1) disconnect   a) troublesome
2) incessant   b) scoured
3) obesity   c) continual
4) scrubbed   d) give up
5) prestigious   e) exulted
6) impairs   f) fatness
7) forgo   g) honored
8) bothersome   h) influential
9) esteemed   i) weakens
10) vaunted   j) detach

B. Now, choose five of the words from the left column and write five sentences below using each of those words in a sentence. You may change the form of the words.
a) _____
b) _____
c) _____
d) _____
e) _____

Classroom Discussion Questions
Discuss the questions below with your classmates. Give your reasons.

1. Why is stress increasing in our society?
2. How much time do you need to sleep at night?
3. Has an insufficient amount of sleep ever impaired your judgment or made you forgetful? If yes, give a specific example.
4. Why do you not you use up all your vacation time every year?
5. Are there any repercussions at your company if you use all of your vacation time?
6. How can Japanese people become happier?

Write discussion questions for class discussions based on the topic in the article. Next, ask your classmates your questions and make sure they give reasons.

1. _____
2. _____
3. _____
4. _____

I'm so Tired, My Mind is on the Blink
Lesson Notes

_____

Today's Vocabulary

Words	Synonym	Antonym	Definition

Collocations/Phrases	Definition

What did I learn today?
_____

What do I need to improve?
_____

My homework for next class
_____

© David Baird

LIFO

Warm Up

Training Survey

Fill in the survey below. Use the last training you attended and rate it by putting a check mark √ in front of your answer.

1. How would your rate this training for meeting your needs?
   _____ Excellent _____ Acceptable _____ Unsatisfactory _____ Poor
2. How would you rate the trainer or trainers' overall skills?
   _____ Excellent _____ Acceptable _____ Unsatisfactory _____ Poor
3. Was the trainer knowledgeable?
   _____ Very Knowledgeable _____ Knowledgeable _____ Not Very familiar
   _____ Clueless
4. Did the trainer communicate clearly and effectively?
   _____ Very Effective _____ Effective _____ Not Very Effective
   _____ I could not follow him/her at all.
5. Was the training well organized?
   _____ Excellent _____ Satisfactory _____ Unsatisfactory _____ Poor
6. How would you rate the quality of the information presented?
   _____ Excellent _____ Satisfactory _____ Unsatisfactory _____ Poor
7. How would you rate the quality of the training materials?
   _____ Excellent _____ Satisfactory _____ Unsatisfactory _____ Poor
8. Were the materials and research current?
   _____ Yes _____ No _____ Don't Know _____ Not Applicable
9. Were the training activities appropriate?
   _____ Yes _____ No _____ Don't Know _____ Not Applicable
10. Did you feel free to ask questions?
    _____ Yes _____ No _____ Not Applicable
11. Were your questions answered to your satisfaction?
    _____ Yes _____ No _____ Not Applicable
12. Have your skills/knowledge increased as a result of the training
    _____ Yes _____ No _____ Don't Know _____ Not Applicable
13. Will you be able to apply what you learned to your job?
    _____ Yes _____ No _____ Don't Know _____ Not Applicable
14. Would you recommend this training to your friends or colleagues?
    _____ Yes _____ No _____ Don't Know _____ Not Applicable
15. How would you rate this training overall?
    _____ Excellent _____ Satisfactory _____ Unsatisfactory _____ Poor
16. What did you like best about the training?
    _____
    _____
17. What did you like the least about the training?
    _____
    _____
18. What improvements would you suggest?
    _____
    _____

Training Skills

Prepare for the class a skill you can teach your classmates. For example, you can teach them how to swing a golf club or how to make an omelet. The choice is yours. Your teacher will tell you how much time you have to teach the skill.

LIFO

There is an accounting technique used in managing inventory and finance called LIFO which stands for last-in first-out, meaning that the most recently produced items are recorded as sold first. Staff training in most companies is also often LIFO, as it is the last thing a company puts into practice and is the first thing that is cut out when the company is looking for cost savings. However, this is a false economy as cutting training may save money in the short term, but it will be more costly in the end.

Training while costly has its benefits, some direct and obvious and others that are more of a by-product. The obvious benefits for training are employees gaining new skills that can contribute more to the business as they could learn how to be more productive, introduce new processes, techniques and technology. Training will also give the company a competitive advantage as the workers can acquire skills, which the competition may not have. Staying ahead of the competition is imperative for a business to be sustainable.

The additional and indirect benefits of training are increased job satisfaction and morale among employees. A training and development program creates more efficient employees who require less supervision and need less detailed instructions. It also enhances a company's image by making it more attractive to potential employees. Prospective employees will look favorably upon a corporation that nurtures its employees and offers them opportunities to develop and grow. Other benefits are lower overall employee turnover, less absenteeism and more internal department communication.

If a company recognizes the above benefits as essential, then the next challenge is how does an organization measure the benefits of training? Training costs money, so human resources managers have to justify the expense. Management can usually see the return from hard skills training such as learning a new computer language, machine operating or bookkeeping. As these skills are measurable and usually give an immediate return, supporting a hard skill training program is not too problematic.

However, if the hard skill training is lengthy such as learning a foreign language or getting an advanced degree, an organization might balk at supporting it because investing time and money on long-term training is daunting. An additional impediment is some companies' fear employees will leave after completing their training. Another reason is the people in charge of paying for the training do not have a long-term plan in place for the newly trained employees. This short-term thinking can lose employees who have training needs that require long-term commitment. Training cuts signal the opportunity to develop and grow as being curtailed and slipping away.

The next predicament is sending employees to obtain soft skills such as leadership, communication or organization skills. Measuring the return on investment (ROI) for soft skills is next to impossible yet they are essential skills that an organization needs its employees to possess for the company to succeed.

The answer to this quandary is easier said than done. To justify training costs, the HR department must measure performance by creating key performance's indicators (KPI) against the stated training, learning and development objectives. Nevertheless, how do you accurately measure leadership development? How do you measure something now that you will not see the results for another three to five years? Creating KPIs that can gauge the usefulness of soft skills training, be traceable, and relate to a meaningful target causes HR managers to lose sleep.

Even so, training is crucial and a cut in company training is a false economy. Companies that have a poor training program, usually fall behind their competitors, are less profitable and have high staff turnover. They may save money in the short run, but in the end, they lose.

© David Baird

LIFO Activity Sheet

True or False Quiz
Based on the reading, circle whether the statements are true or false.
1. LIFO stands for last-in, flake out — True/False
2. A false economy means saving money at the end but results in more money being spent at the beginning. — True/False
3. The clear benefits for training are employees gaining new skills that can contribute more to the business. — True/False
4. Training will give a business a competitive advantage as the staff can obtain expertise, which the competition may not have. — True/False
5. An indirect benefit of training is letting staff getting together to complain. — True/False
6. A training program helps keep employees in the company. — True/False
7. Most organizations support lengthy hard skill training. — True/False
8. Some companies worry about their staff leaving after completing their training. — True/False
9. Most firms have a plan on where to place their newly trained employees. — True/False
10. Creating a KPI to accurately measure training is often nearly impossible. — True/False

Vocabulary Matching Activity
A. Match the words from the reading on the left with the similar meaning words on the right.

1. by-product
2. imperative
3. sustainable
4. nurtures
5. absenteeism
6. balk
7. daunting
8. impediment
9. predicament
10. justify
11. traceable
12. gauge

a) crucial
b) validate
c) discouraging
d) outgrowth
e) measure
f) barrier
g) renewable
h) observable
i) non-attendance
j) quandary
k) back off
l) cultivates

B. Now, choose five of the words from the left column and write four sentences below using each of those words in a sentence. You may change the form of the words.

a) _____
b) _____
c) _____
d) _____
e) _____

Classroom Discussion Questions
Discuss the questions below with your classmates. Give your reasons.

1. If you needed to cut costs in your company, what would you suggest?
2. How good is your company's training program?
3. What training does your company need to add?
4. Which do you need more soft skills or hard skills training?
5. Can you think of any training benefits not mentioned in the article?
6. Why do companies balk in investing in training?
7. What makes a good trainer?
8. What makes a good training program?
9. How do you accurately measure leadership development?
10. How do you measure something now that you will not see the results for another three to five years?

Write discussion questions for the class based on the topic in the article.

a) _____
b) _____
c) _____
d) _____

LIFO Lesson Notes

_____
_____
_____
_____
_____
_____
_____
_____
_____
_____
_____

Today's Vocabulary

Words	Synonym	Antonym	Definition

Collocations/Phrases	Definition

What did I learn today?
_____
_____
_____
_____

What do I need to improve?
_____
_____
_____
_____

My homework for next class
_____
_____
_____

Help Wanted, But Only If...

Warm Up

Classroom Discussion Questions

1. At what age is someone too old?
2. If you were offered the chance to live your life again, would you?
3. Would you agree that you are as old as you feel? Is age just a number?
4. Which celebrity has aged gracefully?
5. Which celebrity do you think fails at looking younger than they are?

Old vs. Young Activity

Group the character traits below on whether you think they are old or young characteristics. Write your answers under the Old/Young headings below.

confident	energetic	ambitious	diligent
tough	enthusiastic	optimism	considerate
funny	thoughtful	spontaneous	courteous
cynical	generous	cautious	sluggish
cautious	impulsive	cranky	arrogant
handsome	pretty	wise	shy
careless	lazy	vain	clever

Old	Young

Vocabulary Finding Activity

A. Find words in the article that have a similar meaning to the words below.

1. re-examination _____
2. inconsistency _____
3. stressed _____
4. treasure _____
5. growing old _____
6. elegantly _____
7. adjust _____
8. has-beens _____
9. forgiven _____
10. presumptions _____
11. bigotry _____
12. eager _____

B. Choose four of the words that you have found in the article from the above vocabulary exercise and write four sentences below using each of those words in a sentence.

a) _____
b) _____
c) _____
d) _____

Expression Definition Activity

Scan the article for the following expressions and guess the meanings for the following expressions.

fountains of wisdom _____

inevitable onslaught of time _____

standard operating procedure _____

coded language _____

Help Wanted, But Only If...

At what age is someone too old? Is it when their first grey hair appears or is it when they turn 40? Age is becoming an important question, as the labor force is getting older and people are staying healthier and active into their later years, so a reassessment of the role of older workers is required.

A contradiction exists in many societies in regards to the elderly. Older people are supposed to be treated with respect and should be seen as fountains of wisdom, which is especially emphasized in Confucian societies like Japan, Korea, and China.

Still those same countries also cherish youth with many older people trying to withstand the inevitable onslaught of time. There are 70-year-old Japanese politicians vainly dying their hair black and Taiwanese men spending time and money on beauty treatments that were once exclusively only for women. Aging gracefully is not the standard operating procedure.

Age is also playing a factor in hiring practices. For example as firms need to be more flexible, they have realized that they need to quickly fill in gaps in their skills. Since there is a limited pool of talented young workers, companies have to look at older workers. This creates a problem, as many firms do not want to hire older workers.

Many employers see older workers as less productive, more expensive, and difficult to train. They are dinosaurs who cannot adapt to the new technology and lack energy. Other myths that employers claim are that older workers need more sick days, they are more expensive and they do not take direction from younger managers.

Not to hire someone based on age, is called ageism and is a form of discrimination. In Japan, ageism appears bluntly in jobs ads where employers state they are looking for someone in their twenties or simply, young person wanted. While these ads are legal in Japan, it is illegal in Europe or North America.

That is not to say that ageism does not exist in other countries. Two American scientists called ageism "the most socially condoned" form of prejudice. Many foreign companies mask their ageism practices by using coded language in their ads and making inferences in the job interview. Some coded language examples are, "We seek enthusiastic employees for a young company" or "The candidate should have a fresh, youthful outlook."

In a job interview, interviewers will ask the candidate about being the proper fit for a new business environment or if he or she is up to date with the latest technology. The interviewer will also insert the most current slang or refer to the latest fad to see if the applicant understands. Perhaps the interviewer may remark, "With your experience, you should be in a more senior position," or "You seem overqualified." The candidate will leave the interview feeling that they are not wanted at that particular company.

Ageism is probably most prevalent in the IT industry where industry leaders such as Facebook CEO Mark Zuckerberg proclaims, "Young people are just smarter," or Vinod Khosla, a co-founder of Sun Microsystems, states, "People over the age of 45 basically die in terms of new ideas." Now when computer engineers approach 35, they anxiously start looking in the mirror for signs of aging.

What the tech industry often forgets is that with age comes wisdom. Research on Nobel Prize winners and successful entrepreneurs, shows that people in their 40s and older are often more productive and creative and than people in their twenties. If a company truly wants to be successful hiring quality people, it needs to look past the applicant's age and look at the person.

© David Baird

Help Wanted, But Only If... Activity Sheet

True and False Quiz
Based on the reading, circle whether the statements are true or false.
1. Older people should not be treated with respect. — True/False
2. Many Japanese politicians are aging gracefully. — True/False
3. Companies do not want to hire older workers because old people are constantly ill. — True/False
4. Ageism is a type of prejudice. — True/False
5. Ageism exists in all countries, but some societies hide it better than others do. — True/False
6. Coded language is often used to hide ageism in hiring practices. — True/False
7. The interviewer will also drop the most current slang on the applicant's foot. — True/False
8. Ageism is seldom seen in the IT industry. — True/False
9. Young people are often more productive and creative than old people. — True/False

Vocabulary Matching Activity
A. Match the words from the reading on the left with the similar meaning words on the right.

1. hire
2. myths
3. mask
4. up to date
5. insert
6. fad
7. remark
8. overqualified
9. slang
10. prevalent
11. anxiously

a) include
b) comment
c) too skilled
d) jargon
e) untruths
f) hide
g) widespread
h) employ
i) fearfully
j) trend
k) current

B. Now, choose six of the words from the left column and write six sentences below using each of those words in a sentence.

a) _____
b) _____
c) _____
d) _____
e) _____
f) _____

Classroom Discussion Questions
Write discussion questions based on the article. Next, ask your classmates your questions and make sure they give coherent explanations.

1. _____
2. _____
3. _____
4. _____
5. _____

Discuss the questions below with your classmates. Give your reasons.

1. Do you think ageism is a major problem?
2. How can the government stop age discrimination?
3. Why don't firms want to hire old people?
4. Would you feel comfortable reporting to someone younger than you?
5. How do you keep yourself up-to-date?
6. Do people over the age of 45 die in terms of new ideas?
7. Does wisdom come with age?
8. Why is hiring someone who is overqualified a bad thing?

Help Wanted, But Only If... Lesson Notes

Today's Vocabulary

Words	Synonym	Antonym	Definition

Collocations/Phrases	Definition

What did I learn today?

What do I need to improve?

My homework for next class

© David Baird

Human Resources Vocabulary Review

Sentence Scramble
Unscramble the words and put them in the correct order to make a proper sentence.

1. still/The/business/persists/myth/nice/ guys/cannot/that/succeed.

2. You/have/Jeff Bezos/succeed/to/a/Steve Jobs/do/not/ rude/jerk/like/to/be/or.

3. company/a/sign/of/low/absenteeism/morale/is/High.

4. The/ business/does/profile/friendly/low key/not/often/of/their/media/ CEOs/the/not/hear/about /and/so/we/do/them.

5. imperative/It/that/we/is/our/staff/reassess/training

6. been/pay/lack/of/complaining/about/and/paltry/perks/their/some/Employees/have.

7. find/aging/task/gracefully/I/to/be/a/daunting.

8. fountain/not/dinosaur/I/an/want/to/be/a/esteemed/of/wisdom.

9. my/job/last/At/was/interview/was/coded/I/that/heard/I/language/too/was/old.

10. The/interviewer/stated/I/last/was/position/overqualified/the/for/

Vocabulary Activity 1

A. Choose the word in each row that has a different meaning from the other words.

1. slang	jargon	standard	lingo	vernacular
2. rare	ubiquitous	prevalent	widespread	common
3. scrutiny	analysis	skimming	examination	inspection
4. impressive	prestigious	ordinary	celebrated	notable
5. vital	paramount	crucial	insignificant	essential
6. incessant	intermittent	relentless	nonstop	continuous
7. brainless	stupid	quick	dim	thick
8. adapt	modify	alter	adjust	neglect
9. cherish	adore	treasure	detest	prize
10 madness	balance	insanity	lunacy	hysteria

B. Now, choose six of the words from the table above and write six sentences below using each of those words in a sentence.

a) _____
b) _____
c) _____
d) _____
e) _____
f) _____

Human Resources Vocabulary Review

Vocabulary Activity 2

A. Fill in the blanks in following sentences with the words in the box below.

disconnected		prestigious	bothersome
forgo	incessant	absenteeism	engaged
obesity	balks	diplomatically	absenteeism

1. Japanese media _____ at reporting why there are so few foreign cars in Japan.
2. He does not seem _____ in his work, but rather _____.
3. His _____ complaining is _____
4. _____ is a major health problem in many English-speaking countries.
5. He _____ told the rude hotel guest to _____ ever returning here ever again.
6. Some people overvalue people who attended a _____ university.
7. Some of the common causes of absenteeism include bullying, harassment, burnout, stress and childcare.

B. Fill in the blanks in following sentences with the words in the box below.

scrubbed	retention	bluntly	morale
eroding	paralysis	impair	justify
	tolerate	dissent	

1. There was no need to _____ her actions as everyone thought she did the right thing.
2. The project was _____ because it was too costly.
3. He is very outspoken as he will _____ tell people why they are wrong.
4. The voters' confidence in the government is _____ because of their _____ in the crisis.
5. Alcohol can _____ a person's judgment.
6. The CEO does not _____ _____ so many independent thinking executives have left the company.
7. Staff _____ is very low because of poor morale.

Vocabulary Writing Activity

Now choose ten of the words or phrases from the list below and write ten sentences below using each of those words or phrases in a sentence.

imperative	sustainable	predicament
retention	esteemed	vaunted
garments	swindler	contentious
make someone tick	hypothetical	by product
domain knowledge	manned	disruption
domino effect	embedded	scrutiny

1. _____
2. _____
3. _____
4. _____
5. _____
6. _____
7. _____
8. _____
9. _____
10. _____

© David Baird

Human Resources Review

Reading Comprehension Quiz

Circle your answers based on the articles from the Human Resources section

1. The best way to keep employees is
    a) making the company unstable
    b) increasing t salary
    c) limiting information flow
    d) bullying your staff

2. Numerous studies show that a lack of sleep can
    a) improve judgment
    b) impair judgment,
    c) increase creativity
    d) make people heedful
    .
3. Always correcting people will make someone seen as
    a) a fun guy
    b) a perceptive person
    c) an argumentative coworker
    d) an intelligent colleague

4. High staff turnover _____ a company in its operations
    a) help
    b) promotes
    c) aids
    d) hinders

5. Companies do not like to invest in hard skill training such as ...
    a) learning a foreign language
    b) learning a computer program
    c) accounting concepts
    d) operating machinery

6. Ageism is still an accepted form of _____ when hiring someone.
    a) objectivity
    b) discrimination
    c) impartiality
    d) justice

Discussion Questions

1. What should be the role of the HR department in a company?
2. How can organizations develop an effective workforce through training and performance appraisal?
3. Should HR departments be involved in leading the company and creating strategy?
4. What do HR professionals usually succeed at doing?
5. What do HR professionals usually fail at doing?
6. What factors are important to recruit quality employees?
7. What is the reason for employee performance evaluations?
8. Why are many large companies (e.g. Microsoft, Accenture, GE) eliminating their staff evaluation systems?

What Have You Learned So Far?

Write your thoughts on what the most interesting, most surprising, most controversial topic that you have discussed from the Human Resources Section.

Two Sides of the Coin

Warm Up

Article Prediction

Just read the first sentence from the article, which is below. After reading it and looking at the title, what do you think the article is about? Write down your prediction below.

Every year, all over the world, there are numerous IT conferences where the shakers and movers of the IT industry assert the importance of the newest advancement and what new opportunities are arising.

_____
_____
_____

Reading Comprehension Activity

After reading the article, answer the following questions.

1. What has been stated since the start of the Industrial Revolution?
2. What diseases are mentioned in the article?
3. What are scientists wondering about?
4. Name three health risks caused by computer usage.
5. How do shy people use technology?

Pros and Cons Activity

List the pros and cons of computers and the Internet.

Pros	Cons

Which One Are You?

How would you rate yourself in relation to technology? Choose one of the categories below and explain your choice..

Technological Utopian: You believe that advances in science and technology will eventually bring about a utopia.
Geek: You are interested in digital technology functions more than its application.
Innovator: You are the first to try new ideas, processes, or goods and services.
Technophile: You love advanced technology
Early Adopter: You are an early customer of a given company, product, or technology and considered a trendsetter.

Early majority: You try new ideas and technology only if you seen that it is successful.
Late majority: You only use something if a friend has recommended it to you.
Laggard: You only use something new because you are forced to.
Technophobe: You have a strong fear about the effects of advanced technology.
Luddite: You are a strong opponent of industrial change or innovation.

Two Sides of the Coin

Every year, all over the world, there are numerous IT conferences where IT industry movers and shakers assert the importance of the newest advancement and what new opportunities are arising. The underlying message preached by these technological utopians is technology is great and it will create a paradise on Earth.

This type of pronouncement is not new, as it has been stated since the advent of the Industrial Revolution. In general, it is true as technology has been a boon for society as the quality of life has improved for billions of people. Advancements in agriculture and medicine have fed more people and allowed people to live longer. Information is dispersed easier and faster so ideas and technology flows throughout the globe.

However, there are two sides to every coin, for each technological advancement that betters society; there has been another one that has harmed society. In the 20th century, great medical advancements were made with development of penicillin, insulin, and a variety of vaccines for diseases such as polio, measles and the whooping cough. At the same time, man created terrible weapons such as mustard gas, napalm, cluster bombs and the atomic bomb.

At the end of the 20th century, the PC and the Internet were invented, which has allowed information to flow much more freely, which has helped everyone from researchers studying DNA to grade school students doing a school paper on butterflies. Global markets are easier to access and friends can easily stay in touch. Computers have helped businesses with accounting software and spreadsheets, which saved countless long nights and improved accuracy.

To make it even easier, the world now has Wi-Fi, smart phones and tablets so it can stay connected no matter the location or time. However, as these devices use up more of people's time, some scientists are wondering on how people's constant use of technology is affecting the body, social skills and the brain.

The health side effects of excessive computer usage can be weight gain, poor blood circulation and bad sleeping habits. Other common computer-related injuries are neck, shoulder, arm and back pain, headaches, and carpal tunnel syndrome that are caused by poorly designed workstations and bad work habits. There is also computer vision syndrome, which is group of eye and vision-related problems that result from prolonged computer, tablet, and smart phone usage.

The diminishing of social skills is something that commentators often worry about the most. Critics are witnessing more people concerned with the texts on their smart phones than on the person in front of them. Technology also lets shy people to lose themselves and escape from reality. Scientists are stating that the overall result is computer users are becoming more socially isolated and awkward due to being stuck in front of PCs and relying on them as a means of communications. Furthermore, other studies show that the isolation has made people exhibit less patience and lack empathy.

How the computer affects the brain is just being studied now. Dr. Maryanne Wolf, an American neuroscientist believes the Internet is damaging people's ability to read for longer periods of time and understand passages in greater depth. As most articles on the Internet are short and require less focus, many individuals are losing the ability to read a complex novel or passages of text that require extended periods of concentration. The result is that in the future a large part of the population will be unable to understand anything that requires prolonged concentration and focus.

For all the benefits of computers, the Internet and portable devices created by very intelligent men and women, an unintended consequence could be a dumber population. As the anonymous Internet quote goes, "I fear the day that technology will surpass our human interaction. The world will have a generation of idiots."

© David Baird

Two Sides of the Coin Activity Sheet

Summarize this Article
Try to summarize this article in three sentences or less
_____
_____
_____

True and False Quiz
Based on the reading, choose whether the statements are true or false.
1. There are numerous IT conferences where influential IT people promote the newest technological advancements. — True/False
2. An implied message at IT conferences is that technology will improve society. — True/False
3. Advancements in agriculture and medicine have allowed for starvation and longer mortality. — True/False
4. In the last century, humanity invented mustard gas, napalm, and the A-bomb. — True/False
5. The Internet has mainly helped grade school students do school papers. — True/False
6. Computers have made life easier for businesses with accounting software. — True/False
7. Healthy side effects of computer use can be getting fat and poor sleeping habits. — True/False
8. An unintended consequence of computers could be a stupider population. — True/False

Vocabulary Match Activity
A. Match the words from the reading to synonyms on the left

1. shakers
2. underlying
3. preached
4. boon
5. dispersed
6. vaccines
7. usage
8. reality
9. diminishing
10. isolated
11. empathy
12. prolonged
13. surpass
14. anonymous

a) advocated
b) compassion
c) employment
d) the here and now
e) declining
f) exceed
g) benefit
h) nameless
i) disseminated
j) lengthy
k) intrinsic
l) preventive medicine
m) cut off
n) influencers

B. Now, choose six of the words on the left column and write six sentences below using each of those words in a sentence. You may change the form of the words.
Example: Her bad behavior has *isolated* her from everyone in the office.

a) _____
b) _____
c) _____
d) _____
e) _____
f) _____

Classroom Discussion Questions
Discuss the questions below with your classmates. Give your reasons.
1. Do you follow the newest changes in technology?
2. Which technology needs to be invented?
3. Which technology do you think should never have been invented?
4. How much do you use a computer or portable device every day?
5. What new technology do you dislike?
6. What new technology do you love?
7. Overall, has technology made the world a better place?
8. When do you want to be disconnected to the Internet?

Two Sides of the Coin Lesson Notes

Today's Vocabulary

Words	Synonym	Antonym	Definition

Collocations/Phrases	Definition

What did I learn today?

What do I need to improve?

My homework for next class

Geeks vs. Suits
Warm Up

Classroom Discussion Questions
1. How would you describe a geek?
2. Do you consider yourself to be a geek?

Tech Acronyms Activity
Write down on the right side the meaning of the following computer acronyms.

1. CPU   _____
2. GUI   _____
3. URL   _____
4. SMS   _____
5. RSS   _____
6. FAQ   _____

Vocabulary Finding Activity
A. Find words in the article that mean the following.

1. nerds   _____
2. acquire   _____
3. establishment   _____
4. cooperation   _____
5. unreservedly   _____
6. cure-all   _____
7. disagreement   _____
8. promoting   _____
9. disposition   _____
10. income   _____
11. expected   _____
12. counterbalance _____

B. Now, choose six of the words you have found in the article from the above activity and write six sentences below using each of those words in a sentence.

a) _____
b) _____
c) _____
d) _____
e) _____
f) _____

Computer History
Match the important moments in the history of the Internet and the PC besides the dates.

1. 1973   a) The Internet is fully commercialized in the U.S.

2. 1975   b) Apple releases the Macintosh.

3. 1976   c) Apple founded by Steve Wozniak, Steve Jobs and Ronald Wayne.

4. 1981   d) Tim Berners Lee implements the first successful communication between an HTTP client and server via the Internet.

5. 1984   e) Jeff Bezos starts Amazon.

6. 1989   f) Altair 8800, a PC computer kit selling for $400 from MITS, introduced in Popular Electronics, sells over 10,000 units in its first month.

7. 1990   g) IBM starts selling its own PC with MS-DOS, which becomes the industry standard

8. 1994   h) The first Internet search engine developed at McGill University

9. 1995   i) Dot-com bubble reaches its peak.

10. 2000   j) Xerox Alto, developed at Xerox PARC, is the first computer to use a mouse, the desktop metaphor, and a GUI.

Geeks vs. Suits

Since the advent of the PC and the Internet, their existence has raised many issues that are continuously being debated. What should be done about cyber-bullying, illegally downloading music and videos? How can a company use the PC and the Internet to make money? Is the Internet a new forum for freedom for everyone to access information or a new marketplace to make millions? What should be free?

Since the early days of PC development in the 1970s in Silicon Valley, an argument arose on how the computer should be used; to make money or to serve humanity. When any revolutionary technology appears, people often debate whether it a panacea for humanity's ills or just the latest moneymaker?

Silicon Valley is close to San Francisco, the center of America's 1960s counter-culture movement. The counter-culture philosophy of sharing, rejecting conventional social customs such as traditional authority and little desire for material wealth, strongly influenced the first developers of the PCs. Many of the initial developments of the PC happened at the Homebrew Computer Club in Silicon Valley, which allowed for an open exchange of ideas that went on at its biweekly meetings, and its club newsletter. There was considerable collaboration and belief in open source systems than there was in competition.

When the money started to arrive, then the competition started to come. Suddenly every computer engineer wanted to be rich and own stock options. Even with the large sums of money available, there are still many developers who want to create free technology, which has resulted in Wikipedia, Linux and OpenOffice.org.

Even within the computer companies, counter-culture ideals continue. Most of the major software and IT companies have a relaxed dress code, free snacks and meals, recreation facilities and innovative looking offices. They see a less structured office environment and a fun work place as keys to encouraging creativity. The CEOs reject the look of traditional authority such as Mark Zuckerberg wearing a hoodie instead of a suit or having company slogans such as "Don't be evil."

However, none of these companies can run on love as they all need money. It is the need for money that creates a conflict between the suits (corporate types) and the geeks (the engineers). Investors, the people with the money, look for people to run companies who have discipline, the proper temperament and a conventional business background to manage a company on a day-to-day basis.

Now sometimes when the suits are in charge, the company can become quite successful. Meg Whitman, a Harvard Business School graduate and Disney executive, was hired in 1998 to be E-Bay's CEO. She did a marvelous job of overseeing the growth of E-Bay from 4 million dollars a year in annual revenue to 8 billion dollars a year.

On the other hand, sometimes the results are not positive. In 1983, Apple hired John Sculley, a successful Pepsi marketing executive to be their CEO. The Apple board envisioned Sculley bringing a mature and winning approach to a fast-growing company that was being run by an inexperienced Steve Jobs. Unfortunately, Sculley's marketing talents did not compensate for his poor product management knowledge as he backed many technologies that failed. As a result, Apple in his last few years started to slide which took them a few years to recover.

In technology-driven companies, there will always be a fight between the suits and the geeks. IT engineers want to create and build while the business people have to find a way to pay for it. Success comes when there are suits who understand the product or geeks who understand how to make money.

© David Baird

Geeks vs. Suits Activity Sheet

True and False Quiz
Based on the reading, circle whether the statements are true or false.

1. The Internet's primary goal is to be a marketplace. — True/False
2. The PC was primarily developed in the 1970s in Death Valley, California. — True/False
3. When new technology appears, many people believe it will cure their sicknesses. — True/False
4. Part of the counter-culture philosophy means sharing and tolerating non-conformity. — True/False
5. Many computer engineers wanted to be rich and have stock options soon after the PC became popular. — True/False
6. Many computer companies try to encourage creativity by having a more rigid workplace. — True/False
7. Investors want senior management to be mainly creative and good motivators. — True/False
8. Internet companies run on love, not money. — True/False
9. Meg Whitman was a successful CEO while John Sculley was not. — True/False
10. Successful companies are run by CEOs who understand the business and know how to earn money. — True/False

Geek or Suit
With a partner, decide whether the following business leaders are geeks or suits. Write your answer beside each one.

Hiroshi Mikitani	Jeff Bezos
(Rakuten founder)	(Amazon founder)
Michael Dell	Mark Zuckerburg
(Founder of Dell)	(Facebook CEO)
Bill Gates	Tim Cook
(Co-Founder Microsoft)	(Apple CEO)
Masayoshi Son	Larry Ellison
(Softbank founder)	(Oracle CEO)
Tomoko Namba	Sergey Brin
(DENA founder)	(Google Co-founder)

Classroom Discussions Questions
Write discussion questions for class discussions based on the topic in the article. Next, ask your classmates your questions and make sure they give reasons.

1. _____
2. _____
3. _____
4. _____
5. _____
6. _____

Additional Questions for Discussion
Discuss the questions below with your classmates. Give your reasons.

1. How can a company make money on the Internet?
2. Is the Internet a new foundation of freedom for everyone to access information or is the Internet a new marketplace to make millions?
3. When did you first use a computer? What model was it? What was the OS?
4. Can new technology help make the world a better place?
5. Does having a relaxed dress code, free food, recreation facilities and innovative looking offices make the workplace more creative?
6. How would you change your work environment?

Geeks vs. Suits Lesson Notes

_____
_____
_____
_____
_____
_____
_____
_____
_____
_____
_____
_____

Today's Vocabulary

Words	Synonym	Antonym	Definition

Collocations/Phrases	Definition

What did I learn today?
_____
_____
_____

What do I need to improve?
_____
_____
_____

My homework for next class
_____
_____
_____

1984 May Still Be Coming

Warm Up

Classroom Discussion Questions
1. Do you worry about your privacy?
2. Have you joined any social media networks?

Social Media Website Quiz
Match the social networking website with its function

1. Facebook
2. Twitter
3. Foursquare
4. Instagram
5. Sina Weibo
6. Yammer

a) Social Networking for internal use in a company
b) Micro blogging
c) General Social Media site
d) Short messaging platform
e) Location based social media network
f) Photo and video sharing site

Reading Comprehension Activity
Scan the article and answer the following questions
1. Who is Big Brother? _____
2. What is Oceania? _____
3. What is a CCTV camera? _____
4. Which countries are mentioned in the article?
   _____
5. What social media networking websites are mentioned?
   _____

Vocabulary Finding Activity
Find words in the reading that have a similar meaning to the words below.

1. represented   _____   9. prophecy   _____
2. values   _____   10. secretly   _____
3. stir   _____   11. existing   _____
4. significant   _____   12. huge   _____
5. comply   _____   13. product   _____
6. beliefs   _____   14. confidential_____
7. exalt   _____   15. inconsistency_____
8. asserts   _____   16. electing   _____

B. Now, choose seven of the words you have found in the article from the above activity and write seven sentences below using each of those words in a sentence.
a) _____
b) _____
c) _____
d) _____
e) _____
f) _____
g) _____

Social Media Network Company
A. With a partner, create a new social media network. Do not forget to name it.
Try to answer these questions when creating your website.
- What is the function of the network?
- What are its features?
- How is it helpful?
- How is it fun to use?
- Who is the target audience?
- How can it make money?

B. Next, convince the class to join your new social network.

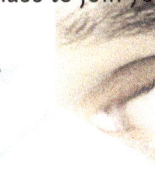
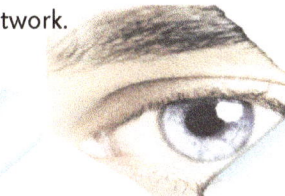
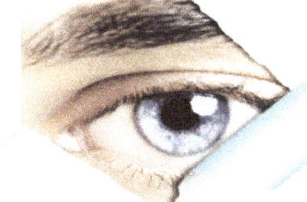

1984 May Still Be Coming

Over 60 years ago, British writer George Orwell wrote a great and prophetic novel called 1984. In 1984, the government of Oceania, which is symbolized by its leader Big Brother, can see everything and controls all information. The government alters history books and newspapers so that the historical records agree with current party principles. The government goes even further to control people's thinking by destroying words that can inspire people and remind people of freedom and free thought.

Even though the year 1984 has passed, the novel's warning of what the future might hold is still relevant. Governments today are also using many of the tools and techniques that Big Brother used in Nineteen Eighty-Four.

Take for example textbooks. The lead character in 1984, John Smith rewrites history textbooks to conform to the party in power. Today, in China, Japan, the USA and many other countries, textbooks are revised so they can promote the ideology of the people in power. The result is history is often taught to glorify, not to educate about a country's past.

Another example of where Orwell's prediction was quite accurate was the widespread use of closed circuit television cameras (CCTV) to watch people constantly. In London, there are over 10,000 cameras controlled by the government claimed to help prevent crime. Overall, in the UK, it is estimated that there is an average of one camera for every 32 people. One report claims that 70 CCTV cameras would record the average British person on a typical day. However, these cameras have not actually succeeded in lowering crime, but seem just to let Big Brother keep close track of its citizens.

The one thing that Orwell did not predict in 1984 was the invention of the Internet, and its effects on privacy. Who controls the private data is a contentious topic as more and more people are using the Internet, so there is progressively more personal information floating around the World Wide Web. The Internet is a powerful tool to pass and collect information for both governments and companies.

The US government has been found to be clandestinely collecting mountainous amounts of everyone's private data from the Internet. Corporations are now collecting an immense amount of information, which they use to profile their customers, so they can offer customers goods and services based on their profile. As well,  they will sell that information, so personal details are not just used a marketing tool, but also become a commodity. For that reason, what records should be protected and private versus what information should be accessible is widely being debated by politicians, corporations and concerned citizens.

While some people argue about the need for privacy controls on the Internet, many people are giving away very personal details through social media. People are happily posting intimate information on websites like Mixi, Twitter or Facebook. It is a paradox that people want to share private details on the Internet, but at the same time want to remain in complete control of who gets to see the info. The result is people are co-opting own loss of privacy. They should realize that it in a social network's best interest to collect data and mine it.

What would Orwell think of the many people who tell the public where they are on Foursquare, tweet what they are thinking and show photos of who their friends are on Facebook? Obviously, no one knows, but he would probably think we are like the sheep, from one of his other famous books, Animal Farm, who blindly followed their leaders.

© David Baird

1984 May Still Be Coming Activity Sheet

True/False Qui
Based on the reading, circle whether the statements are true or false.

1. Over 60 years ago, George Orwell penned 1984. — True/False
2. The fictional government of Oceania was led by Big Father. — True/False
3. The Oceania government could see and direct everything. — True/False
4. The Oceania government created words that encouraged freedom and free thought. — True/False
5. Many countries use school textbooks to promote their leadership's beliefs. — True/False
6. In London, there are over 100,000 cameras controlled by the government that help stop crime. — True/False
7. Internet companies do not sell their customer's personal information. — True/False
8. What ISP people should choose is the central issue concerning the Internet. — True/False
9. People enjoy giving personal information on social media websites. — True/False
10. If Orwell were alive, he would probably think people are now blindly following what ever their leaders say. — True/False

Pros and Cons Activity
List the pros and cons of joining a social media network then discuss your answers with your classmates.

Pros	Cons

Classroom Discussions Questions
Write discussion questions for class discussions based on the topic in the article. Next, ask your classmates your questions and make sure they give reasons.

a) _____
b) _____
c) _____
d) _____
e) _____
f) _____

Additional Questions for Discussion
Discuss the questions below with your classmates. When answering please give reasons and detailed explanation to support your views. Furthermore, make sure to ask follow up questions to your classmates' responses.

1. Have you ever read 1984? If no, would you like to?
2. Orwell predicted a negative future, a dystopia in 1984. What is your feeling about the future? Are you optimistic or pessimistic?
3. What is your opinion about CCTV cameras?
4. What information should corporations be allowed to collect?
5. Do you ever read science fiction?
6. What are your views about privacy on the Internet?
7. What rules should the government make to protect people's privacy?
8. What information should governments be allowed to collect?
9. Who do you trust more, governments or companies to protect your privacy?
10. What advice would you give people worried about privacy?

1984 May Still Be Coming Lesson Notes

_____
_____
_____
_____
_____
_____
_____
_____
_____
_____

Today's Vocabulary

Words	Synonym	Antonym	Definition

Collocations/Phrases	Definition

What did I learn today?
_____
_____
_____

What do I need to improve?
_____
_____
_____

My homework for next class
_____
_____

Noise from the Knowledge

Warm Up

Classroom Discussion Questions
1) Can you give an example of what information is essential and what information is trivial?
2) What trivial information do you often find interesting?
3) What information do you not care about?

Fill in the Blank

| value | bombarded | measured |
| knowledge | opinion | facing |

Fill in the blanks in the sentences with words from the box above.

1. The first problem is to decide what an _____. is and what a fact is.
2. Everyday we are _____ by thousands of bytes of information.
3. Companies are now _____ the problem of deciding what noise is and what knowledge is.
4. Can the _____ of people's work always be _____ by these numbers?
5. However, information and technology cannot replace _____, wisdom and experience.

Vocabulary Match Activity
Match these recently popular business expressions with their definitions

1. corporate synergy
2. KPI
3. EPMS
4. ROI
5. B2B
6. core competency

a) Return on Investment
b) Key Performance Indicator
c) A specific factor that a business sees as central to the way the company works
d) Business to Business transactions
e) Benefit when a company merges with or buys another company
f) Employee Performance Management e System

New Title
After reading the article, create a new title for the article
_____
_____

Reading Comprehension
After reading the article, answer the following questions.

a) What are we bombarded by?
b) What is noise?
c) Who is Clay Shirky?
d) What is the free buffet?

Summarize the Article
Try to summarize this article in three sentences or less.
_____
_____
_____
_____
_____
_____

Noise from the Knowledge

Is it difficult to tell the forest from the trees? The essential from the trivial? Is it hard to separate the signal from the noise? We now live in the Information Age with high-speed Internet access, 24-hour cable news and smart phones keeping us in constant contact. Every day we are bombarded by thousands of bytes of information. Now most of it is noise, trivial information while some of it is knowledge, significant information. However, which is which?

It is important to distinguish between the vapid fluff and useful knowledge as we want to formulate our views based on relevant facts; the facts that matter and not the trivial ones.

People often delude themselves into thinking that their decisions are based on significant facts, not unimportant details. The insignificant is often deemed important and the important is ignored. There are many reasons why people have problems sifting out the noise. Experts have stated that these problems can occur because of a reliance on the quantity of information over quality, too much short-term thinking, personal prejudices and blindly accepting conventional wisdom.

Companies are now facing the problems of deciding what noise is and what knowledge is. In organizations, a major problem is they now have too much data. Computerization has now brought a flood of information that would have drowned most executives thirty years ago. Metrics, EPMS, KPIs, scorecards and dashboards are now the buzzwords in managing people and businesses.

Is relying on numbers wise, especially for managing people? Can the value of people's work always be measured by these numbers? Is this thinking making employers transform employees into robots? Some HR analysts are starting to see managers over relying on numbers and ignoring the personal touch. This over reliance on numerical data has made some managers and executives forget that there staff are people not just cogs in the machine.

Additionally the problem with handling information also exists in marketing. In spite of the Internet giving marketing firms the ability to document every click, purchase and comment so they can target their message based on people's behavior they still struggle. Marketing firms grapple with differentiating their message from the millions of other messages being sent using the same technology

However, the problem is just not solely concerned with how a business manages its people or markets its products. Clay Shirky, a respected American commentator on the IT industry has stated that, the problem with information is not information overload but rather filter failure. In traditional knowledge management, the focus has been on quantity, not quality. Too much information is collected so there is now too much noise.

Therefore, the real problem for organizations is to decide on what the filter setting should be. Now this takes real self-discipline and courage. Discipline in that it is so easy to collect immense amounts of information yet companies have to be disciplined to pull themselves away from the free buffet and only take what is necessary. Courage in that the company may have to ignore the latest and hottest KPI that is being trumpeted by the business media and follow what it knows to be best.

Companies must remember that the information and the technology, which brought it, are great as a tool to augment human ability. However, information and technology cannot replace knowledge, wisdom and experience.

© David Baird

Noise from the Knowledge Activity Sheet

True/False Quiz
Based on the reading, circle whether the statements are true or false.
1) In the Disinformation Age, we now have high-speed Internet access, 24-hour cable news and smart phones to keep us in constant contact. — True/False
2) People frequently deceive themselves into thinking that their decisions are based on significant facts. — True/False
3) There is a large reliance on the quality of information over the quantity. — True/False
4) Too much short term thinking, personal prejudices and blindly accepting conventional wisdom affect people from deciding what is important. — True/False
5) KPI and EPMS mean the same thing. — True/False
6) Marketing firms can easily differentiate their message from others because of the Internet. — True/False
7) Clay Shirky says the problem is filter failure, not information overload. — True/False
8) Companies need to collect immense amounts of information to determine what is necessary. — True/False
9) Information and technology will never replace wisdom and experience. — True/False

Vocabulary Match Activity
A. Match the words from the reading to synonyms on the left

1. bombarded
2. vapid fluff
3. delude
4. sifting
5. dashboards
6. grapple
7. buzzwords
8. differentiate
9. trumpeted
10. augment

a) sorting through
b) distinguish
c) flooded
d) trivial nonsense
e) enhance
f) proclaimed
g) mislead
h) unified displays
i) catchphrases
j) wrestle

B. Now, choose five of the words on the left column and write five sentences below using each of those words in a sentence. You may change the word form.
Example: I am *grappling* with a motivation problem.

a) _____
b) _____
c) _____
d) _____
e) _____

Classroom Discussion Questions
Discuss the questions below with your classmates. Give your reasons.
1. Can the value of people's work always be measured by metrics?
2. Is this thinking making employers transform employees into robots?
3. Has the reliance on numbers stopped managers in aiding their staff in performing to the best of their ability?
4. How can advertising make itself different from other messages?
5. Do you agree with Clay Shirky that filter failure is a major problem, not information overload?
6. Has information and technology replaced knowledge, wisdom and experience?

Write discussion questions for class discussions based on the topic in the article. Next, ask your classmates your questions and make sure they give reasons.

a) _____
b) _____
c) _____
d) _____

Noise from the Knowledge Lesson Notes

_____
_____
_____
_____
_____
_____
_____
_____
_____
_____

Today's Vocabulary

Words	Synonym	Antonym	Definition

Collocations/Phrases	Definition

What did I learn today?
_____
_____
_____
_____

What do I need to improve?
_____
_____
_____
_____

My homework for next class
_____
_____
_____

IT Articles Vocabulary Review

Sounding Natural
Often people when learning a new language make a mistake when choosing words. They choose a word that has a similar meaning but use it in the wrong context.
Example: I denied his suggestion.
The correct sentence is "I rejected his suggestion."

The definition for *reject* is dismiss because someone or something is inadequate, unacceptable, or faulty while the definition for *deny* is refuse to give (something requested or desired) to (someone). These errors can be sometimes caused by using native language (such as Japanese) to English dictionaries, which do often show in what context the words are used.

Word Choice Activity 1
Choose the right word for the sentences below
1. Jesus's rising from the dead, his resurrection, is a necessary part of Christian **belief/view**.
2. A good teacher is able to **claim/assert** authority when required in the classroom.
3. It is **important/significant** to differentiate about/between the platforms of both candidates.
4. The idea of this being my new **reality/real world** terrifies me.
5. This book **promotes/ recommends** his views on capitalism, economics and business.
6. Weekends should be **confidential/private** time for all of employees.
7. I will need a second **income/ revenue** unless I get a raise soon.
8. He **inspired/excited** people to do bigger and better things.
9. She just doesn't have the **temperament/posture** for dealing with fools.
10. It is very difficult to **obtain/take** earthquake insurance in some countries.

Sounding Natural (continued)
Another reason why some non-native speakers have a problem sounding natural is they choose the wrong form of the word. Students often use the noun form of the word when they should be using the verb form.
Example: What do you recommendation for dinner?
The correct sentence is "What do you recommend for dinner."

Word Form Activity
Complete the table with the words from the articles by writing their related forms.

Noun	Verb	Adjective
	delude	
usage		
	differentiate	
	augment	
	XXXXXX	astronomical
		transformative
	glorify	XXXXXX
prediction		
	innovate	
		private
	inspire	
	symbolize	

Word Choice Activity 2
Circle the correct forms of the word in the sentences below.
1. Nassim Taleb believes accurate *predictions/predictability* are impossible to make because there are too many variables.
2. I cannot *differentiate/difference* between an Australian and New Zealand accent.
3. Children should be *vaccine/vaccinated* against common diseases such as mumps, measles and chicken pox.
4. His *isolation/isolated* from society caused him to hate people.
5. Logos are *symbols/symbolic* for products.
6. Her singing was *inspirational/inspiration*.

IT Articles Vocabulary Review

Writing Activity

Now choose seven of the words or phrases from the previous word form activity and write seven sentences below using each of those words in a sentence.
   Example: A *fallacy* is an incorrect argument in logic or debating.

a) _____
b) _____
c) _____
d) _____
e) _____
f) _____
g) _____

Sounding Natural (continued)

The next obstacle for many non-native speakers is not utilizing collocations in their speech. Collocations are the usual matching or combining of a particular word with another word or words that are commonly used together in English. Think of collocations as words that usually go together.

One example is the phrase strong tea, which is used instead of powerful tea.
There are several different types of collocations. Collocations can be adjective + adverb, noun + noun, verb + noun and so on. Below you can see seven types of collocation in sample sentences.

1. Adverb + adjective
She is making an *exceptionally useful* contribution to the company's bottom line.
Are you *fully aware* of the implications of your action?
2. Adjective + noun
I thought the whole idea was just a *foolish* and *dangerous delusion*.
Japan will never undergo a *radical transformation*.
3. Noun + noun
Could you please give our next speaker a big a *round* of *applause?*
IT companies have to always worry about constant *product innovation*.
4. Noun + verb
Vaccines protect children against tuberculosis.
An *argument erupted* at our meeting.
5. Verb + noun
He was *suffering* from *delusions* of grandeur
I want to *make* a *prediction* that solar panels will become more common in Japan.
6. Verb + expression with preposition
We had to return home because we had *run out* of money.
Squeeze the fruit to *test for* ripeness.
7. Phrases
The new appraisal scheme is only a *taste of things to come*.
There's *been a shift in* government *thinking* on genetically-modified food.

Word Choice Activity 3

Choose the correct word in each of the sentences below to make the correct collocation..

1. That word is no longer in *ordinary/common* usage
2. He seemed to be *under/over* the delusion that he would make his fortune within a few years.
3. How do I *teach/explain* a paradox to my friend without getting too complicated?
4. These e-mails are a gross *invasion/attack* of privacy.
5. She *remained/kept* herself almost isolated from her colleagues.
6. It *seems/sees* to be a trivial matter.
7. Accurately measuring language skills poses a *hard/difficult* dilemma for teachers.
8. Where did you *get/come up with* the inspiration for the book?
9. Time is a *precious/costly* commodity.
10. After weeks of overtime, she was starting to *suffer/feel* the strain.
11. The new computer provides *access/admission* to all the files.
12. Egos sometimes hinder *rich/fruitful* collaboration in a project.

IT Discussion Articles Vocabulary Review

Writing Activity
Now choose seven of the words or phrases from below and write seven sentences below using each of those words in a sentence.
Example: I need to **give up** smoking.

astronomical	bombarded	give up	delude	trademark
dispersed	patent	boon	movers and shakers	delude
underlying	paradox	advent	at the same time	dilemma

a) _____
b) _____
c) _____
d) _____
e) _____
f) _____
g) _____

Sounding Natural (continued)
Another problem is that non-native speakers often are confused with words that have a similar sound but often have a much different meaning.

Example: He remained me that I have to work hard to succeed.
The correct sentence is "He reminded me that I have to work hard to succeed. "

Word Choice Activity 4
Circle the correct spelling of the word in the sentences below
1. I think he is very *principaled/principled*.
2. The Wright Brother's *innovation/invention* of the airplane changed transportation.
3. She often *complains/claims* when he comes home late.
4. I don't want to *conform/confirm* to society's rules.
5. She *sifted/shifted* in the chair to get more comfortable.
6. *Laws/lows* are made by politicians.
7. He *brought/bought* potato salad to the picnic.
8. The shirt is very *lose /loose* on me.

Fill in the Blank Activity
Fill in the blanks in the sentences below with the words in the box. You may have to change the word form in the sentence.

vapid fluff	mountainous	transformative	glorify
buzzword	commodity	fallacy	trivial
empathy	usage	progress	relevant

1. He often talked how recovering from cancer was a _____ experience in his life.
2. Japanese variety shows are really just _____
3. He was disappointed that English level had not _____ further after one week of intense study.
4. Too often society _____ greed more than generosity, kindness, and compassion.
5. His questions are always _____ to what is being discussed.
6. Occasionally things that seem _____ are often important.
7. Wheat, oil and corn are important _____ on many major stock exchanges.
8. When I come back from vacation, I usually have a _____ amount of emails to read.
9. Aristotle identified thirteen _____ as errors in logic.
10. Truly listening to someone is one of the most important ways you can show _____.
11. Sometimes, English language _____ does not always follow grammar rules.
12. Twerking, selfie, and whistleblowers have recently been popular _____.

EQ > IQ (Part 1)
Warm Up

Classroom Discussion Questions
1. How do you define success?
2. Do you consider yourself successful?
3. What qualities are needed to be successful?

Personality Adjectives Activity
Complete the statements in the bottom using the adjectives from the list. You may use additional adjectives if none of these adjectives below are suitable.

adaptable	adventurous	aggressive	affectionate
agreeable	ambitious	arrogant	boastful
boring	bossy	brave	broad-minded
calm	careful	charming	communicative
compulsive	compassionate	conscientious	careless
considerate	creative	cunning	decisive
determined	diplomatic	diligent	detached
dishonest	domineering	fussy	friendly
funny	generous	greedy	helpful
honest	independent	intelligent	indecisive
inflexible	interfering	intolerant	irresponsible
jealous	lazy	loyal	moody
narrow-minded	nasty	optimistic	passionate
patronizing	patient	persistent	pessimistic
practical	pro-active	quarrelsome	quick-tempered
quick witted	reliable	resourceful	ruthless
self-confident	selfish	self-disciplined	sensible
sincere	straightforward	stingy	stubborn
timid	thoughtless	tough	touchy
versatile	warmhearted	weak-willed	willing

1. To be successful in my organization, a person should be _____, _____, _____, and _____.
2. I like to work with people who are _____, _____, _____ and _____.
3. I would like my boss to be _____, _____, _____ and _____.
4. A terrible boss is someone who is _____, _____, _____ and _____.
5. I would like people to think that I am _____, _____, _____, and _____.
6. I don't like people who are _____, _____, _____, and _____.
7. The perfect friend would be _____, _____, _____, and _____.
8. To be successful in life, a person should be _____, _____, _____, and _____.

Which Is Most Important?
Of the following four qualities, rank them in the level of importance (1 is the most important, 4 is the least important).

1. _____ Self-management: Manage, control, and adapt our emotions, mood, reactions, and responses
2. _____ Motivation: Apply our emotions so we motivate ourselves to take appropriate action, commit, follow-through, and work toward the achievement of our goals.
3. _____ Empathy: Distinguish how others feel, understand their emotions, and utilize that understanding to relate to others more effectively.
4. _____ Social Skills: Build relationships, relate to others in social situations, lead, negotiate conflict, and work as part of a team.

EQ > IQ

Success is Not in Our Stars (Part 1)

What makes someone successful? Is it their intelligence, their looks, their charm, their blood type or their place of birth? These are questions that countless people have wanted to answer for years. Now for individuals in society who desire to be successful, and richer, an industry has been created to help people do just that.

So if you read this book, listen to that expert, and attend these seminars, you can be a success and all for the price of $19.95. Some of the most popular non-fiction books written over the last 80 years have tried to teach people how to be successful.

So where does success come from? Does success come from being very intelligent and having a high IQ? The short answer is no. The longer answer is that you do need to be somewhat intelligent. An IQ from 110 to 130 is seen as the threshold needed to succeed. Exhaustive studies have shown that very intelligent people with IQs over 140 are not likely to be as successful as someone with an IQ at 120.

So if it is not a high IQ that brings success, then what? A newer theory states that a person needs to have a high emotional intelligence (EQ) in order to do well. The general theory of emotional intelligence states that each person processes information of an emotional nature differently and how they react to it will differ. Having a high EQ will allow someone to be more adaptable to various situations. One problem with EQ is that it has not yet been determined how to measure it exactly.

It may seem counterintuitive that EQ is more important than IQ, but imagine you are at a party, talking to someone very intelligent. This intelligent person may not have great social skills or could be boring. Do you want to continue chatting with them for long? If you were working with them, would you want to deal with them every day? Probably not. The main reason is human beings are social animals and desire to work and interact with people that they like. People often forget that businesses are essentially people, so anything that impacts the effectiveness of people's psyche, judgment or intelligence also impacts the businesses they run or work for.

People with high EQs can perceive and understand emotions better which allows them to see how people are feeling and the complexity of relationships. They can also use and manage their emotions in a positive way and adapt them to different situations such as problem solving or thinking. Lastly, they are able to handle emotions; the emotionally intelligent person can employ all types of emotions, and manage them to achieve intended goals.

A good example of the importance of EQ is with Google the Internet giant. Most people would suppose Google to be more concerned with the IQ than EQ. Google states that its screening process relies on measurable things, like grades and SAT scores that would represent IQ. Nevertheless, at the end of the day, the most important criteria for the hiring process is whether or not they want to work beside the job candidate every day. This is not behavior generally expected from a successful IT company.

Now for people who want to be successful, yet do not possess people skills, do not fret. EQ can be improved, but it takes practice. An important first step is to be interested in other people when meeting them. So at the next party, conference or meeting you attend, spend time asking other people questions. Take the time to see how they react to questions and comments and what their mood is. Keep the conversation on a positive note. Repeating this enough times will build your people skills, which will result in a higher EQ.

By continually practicing this, not only will you increase your EQ, but you will also make a good first impression. As you may know, a good first impression is the first step on the road to success.

EQ > IQ

Activity Sheet

True or False Quiz

Circle whether the statement is true or false based on the reading

1. The most popular fiction books from the last 80 years teach people how to be successful. — True/False
2. An IQ from 125 to 150 is the minimum required to be successful. — True/False
3. EQ theory states that everyone processes information of an emotional nature differently. — True/False
4. Intelligent people almost always have great social skills. — True/False
5. High EQ is more important than high IQ. — True/False
6. People are not sociable and prefer to work alone. — True/False
7. A standard EQ test has been created that people can now take. — True/False
8. People with a high EQ, can understand emotions better which allows them to control other people's feelings. — True/False

Vocabulary Matching Activity

A. Match the words on the left with the synonyms on the right.

1. threshold
2. exhaustive
3. adaptable
4. processes
5. counterintuitive
6. deal with
7. adapt
8. perceive
9. take the time
10. continually

a) adjust
b) flexible
c) thorough
d) recognize
e) constantly
f) contrary to beliefs
g) watch for
h) starting point
i) handle
j) evaluates

B. Now, choose five of the words from the left column and write five sentences below using each of those words in a sentence.
Example: I am on the *threshold* of something great.

a) _____
b) _____
c) _____
d) _____
e) _____

Classroom Discussion Questions

Write discussion questions based on the article. Next, ask your classmates your questions and make sure they give reasons.

1. _____
2. _____
3. _____
4. _____
5. _____

Additional Questions for Discussion

Discuss the questions below with your classmates. Give your reasons.

1. What do you think are the secrets to success?
2. What advice would you give someone who wants to be successful?
3. Do you think possessing a high IQ is important?
4. What is your view about EQ? Do you think EQ is a valid theory?
5. Can people improve their EQ? If yes, how do you think they can do it?
6. How would you rate your EQ?

EQ > IQ (Part 1) Lesson Notes

_____
_____
_____
_____
_____
_____
_____
_____
_____
_____
_____

Today's Vocabulary

Words	Synonym	Antonym	Definition

Collocations/Phrases	Definition

What did I learn today?
_____
_____
_____

What do I need to improve?
_____
_____
_____

My homework for next class
_____
_____
_____

© David Baird

Work Your Tail Off

Warm Up

Classroom Discussion Questions
1. Do you believe hard work leads to success?
2. Who is the hardest working person you know?

How Many Hours Quiz
Circle your guess on the number of hours it takes to do something.
1. How many hours does it take a native English speaker to learn Japanese?
   1000 hours   1700 hours   2200 hours   3400 hours
2. How many hours does it take a native Japanese speaker to learn English?
   1000 hours   1700 hours   2200 hours   3400 hours
3. How long does golfer Tiger Woods train every day?
   4 hours   6 hours   8 hours   12 hours
4. How many hours of total flight time does it take to become a pilot for a major airline?
   400 hours   1500 hours   2500 hours   3000 hours
5. How long does it take to become rich?
   0 hours   500 hours   1000 hours   2500 hours

Vocabulary quiz
A. Fill in the correct word in the blanks below.
1. You can't expect to become a brilliant dancer overnight, but practice makes _____.
   accuracy   achievement   perfect   improvement
2. She is a world-class _____ on butterflies.
   expert   specialist   professional   connoisseur
3. Don't worry if you can't do it at first, it _____ practice.
   makes   does   follows   takes
4. This quiz _____ students practice in using collocations.
   takes   gives   does   follows
5. Many HR managers lack the necessary _____ to scrutinize training programs effectively.
   talent   incompetence   expertise   cunning

Hard Work Quotes
Do you agree with the following quotations? Give your reasons.
1. "A dream doesn't become reality through magic; it takes sweat, determination and hard work."
   Colin Powell
   _____
   _____
   _____

2. "Talent is cheaper than table salt. What separates the talented individual from the successful one is a lot of hard work."   *Stephen King*
   _____
   _____
   _____

3. "Hard work without talent is a shame, but talent without hard work is a tragedy."
   Robert Half
   _____
   _____
   _____

4. "The trouble with opportunity is that it always comes disguised as hard work."
   Herbert Prochnow
   _____
   _____
   _____

Work Your Tail Off

Success is Not in Our Stars (Part 2)

The previous article stated that emotional intelligence (EQ) is important for success. It is not however the only factor. There are many other factors, but the most often asserted one in many cultures is that people need to work hard to be successful.

In Malcolm Gladwell's bestselling book on success *Outliers*, he brings up the 10,000-hour rule as a cornerstone to success. The 10,000-hour rule is based on a study by K. Ander Ericsson, a Swedish psychologist, was first discussed in academic circles in the early 1970s. 10,000 hours is the amount of time someone must do something to be proficient in it which works out to be 20 hours per week of practice for 10 years.

In *Outliers*, Gladwell describes how the Beatles were able to practice and perform much more often than any of their peers as evidence of the 10,000 hours rule veracity. From 1960 to 1962, the Beatles were performing at least 45 hours a week in Hamburg while their contemporaries in England would be lucky to perform 4 hours in a week. After their first Hamburg engagement in 1960, the Beatles were the most skilled band in Liverpool. All members of the Beatles have said that Hamburg is where they honed their skills and matured.

The amount of practice has also been shown to differentiate the ability of violinists. In the early 1990s, some psychologists studied violin students in Berlin, Germany. The violinists were divided into three categories, fair, good and elite. The psychologists examined their practice habits

from childhood to adulthood. The violinists had all taken up the violin when they were around five years old and practiced for a similar amount of time until they reached eight. At that time, their practice time began to differ. The elite started practicing more and remained more dedicated. By twenty, each elite violinist has averaged more than 10,000 hours of practice while the fair performers had only 4,000 hours of practice time. The top violinists had more than double the practice hours of the least capable performers.

Nevertheless, it is not just the amount of hours that separates the great from the fair, but also the type of practice that each person does. To become outstanding, not just countless hours of repetitive training are needed, but also dedication to the right type of practice. New challenges are required in the practice session in order to become great, so a person must try to practice outside their comfort zone. Some experts have labeled this deliberate practice.

Geoff Colvin, author of *Talent is Overrated* stated that deliberate practice is made up of six elements. First, it should be designed to improve performance. Practice must stretch an individual just beyond his current abilities. Second, it has to be repeated a lot. Multiple repetitions will help the task become much easier. Third, feedback on results is required. Someone has to judge whether the performance was good or bad. Next, each practice should demand focus and concentration. This will be hard, and failure will happen so handling failure is important. Failing is not enjoyable, but it is unavoidable as new things are attempted. Finally, the practice needs goals that are about the process of reaching the objective.

The last concept, which is perhaps difficult to understand, can best be explained by two different golfers' approaches to practice. One golfer's training goal is to hit one hundred balls out of a bunker not concerned with the results. A golfer following deliberate practice principles will hit balls out of a bunker until he feels he is confident in his skill to successfully get out of the bunker. The goal is more important than the time or quantity.

In the many things people try, such as learning a new language, mastering an instrument or becoming adept at their job, they must remember the price to be successful is hard work and being determined to stretch themselves. The effort required may seem intimidating but as football coach Vince Lombardi once said, "The only place success comes before work is in the dictionary."

© David Baird

Work Your Tail Off (Part 2)
Activity Sheet

True or False Quiz
Based on the reading, circle whether the statements are true or false.
1. Only Anglo-Saxon culture asserts that hard work is important for success. — True/False
2. 1,000 hours of practice is needed before someone can be an expert. — True/False
3. Malcolm Gladwell used the Beatles as an example of hard work leading to success. — True/False
4. Elite violinists rehearse more than triple the time as mediocre violinists. — True/False
5. The 10,000-hour rule was first discussed in universities in the Seventies. — True/False
6. Deliberate practice consists of seven essentials. — True/False
7. Feedback is a necessity for improvement in the deliberate practice model. — True/False
8. People should always practice from their comfort zone so they will stay confident. — True/False
9. Most golfers enjoy hitting balls out of sand traps. — True/False
10. Hard work is intimidating, but necessary for success. — True/False

Vocabulary Finding Activity
A. Find words in the reading that have a similar meaning.
1. stressed _____
2. raises _____
3. foundation _____
4. equals _____
5. authenticity _____
6. skilled _____
7. preeminent _____
8. committed _____
9. secure position _____.
10. conscious _____
11. guidance _____
12. extend _____
13. attention _____
14. idea _____

B. Now, choose seven of the words you found in the article from the above activity and write seven sentences below using each of those words in a sentence.
Example: *I don't know if my **peers** respect me.*
a) _____
b) _____
c) _____
d) _____
e) _____
f) _____
g) _____

Classroom Discussion Questions
Discuss the questions below with your classmates. Give your reasons.
1. Do you think you have the talent to be a top performer?
2. What have you practiced doing the most? Why? Are you good at it now?
3. What feedback do you give your subordinates or peers?
4. What feedback do you like to receive from your supervisors or peers?
5. How do you feel when you are outside your comfort zone?
6. Why do some people work hard but never succeed?
7. Is there any other way to be successful without working hard?
8. When have you learned from failure?

Write discussion questions based on the article. Next, ask your classmates your questions and make sure they give reasons.
a) _____
b) _____
c) _____
d) _____
e) _____
f) _____

Work Your Tail Off (Part 2) Lesson Notes

_____
_____
_____
_____
_____
_____
_____
_____
_____
_____
_____
_____

Today's Vocabulary

Words	Synonym	Antonym	Definition

Collocations/Phrases	Definition

What did I learn today?
_____
_____
_____
_____

What do I need to improve?
_____
_____
_____
_____

My homework for next class
_____
_____
_____

True Grit (Part 3)
Warm Up

Classroom Discussion Questions
1. How strong is your self-control?
2. Are you mentally tough?

Vocabulary Activity
A. Put the phrases and words under either the tough or soft label.

resolute	sturdy	pliable	inflexible	strong
scaredy cat	determined	gutless	dropout	
gritty	wuss	a hard nut	paper tiger	
chicken hearted	hard as nails	fainthearted	spineless	

Tough | Soft

B. Now choose six of the words or expressions from the above activity and write six sentences below using each of those words in a sentence.
Example: *I think he is a wuss because he did not support me.*

1. _____
2. _____
3. _____
4. _____
5. _____
6. _____

Tough or Soft
Which of these people do you think are tough or soft? Write tough or soft after their name and then explain your reasons to your classmates.

Ken Watanabe _____   Dalai Lama _____
Christine Lagarde _____ Bill Gates _____
Hiroshi Mikitani _____   Barack Obama _____
Ayumi Hamasaki _____   Jeff Bezos _____
Malala Yousafzai _____   Masayoshi Son _____
Xi Jinping _____   Tom Hanks _____
Tsuyoshi Kusanagi _____ Yuri Ebihara _____
Ichiro Ozawa _____   Yu Darvish _____

Reading Comprehension
After reading the article, answer the following questions.

a) What was pointed out in the last two articles?
b) How do gritty people "stay the course?"
c) Where would the Beatles have headed back home to in 1960?
d) What do people have a hard time dealing with these days?

True Grit

Success Is Not In Our Stars (Part 3)

Recently one other quality besides a high EQ and long hours of practice has come to the fore as an important requirement for success: willpower. Willpower is the mental control that people have to control their impulses. Specifically two facets of willpower are seen as necessary grit and self-control. Self-control has been well studied by psychologists since the 1950s, but grit has been only closely researched in the last ten years. Of the two traits, grit is seen as a more important factor to success.

What is grit? A definition for grit, according to Angela Duckworth, a leading psychologist in the study of grit, is the "perseverance and passion for a long-term goal." Someone with grit does not require immediate positive feedback. Gritty individuals stay determined and motivated over long periods despite experiencing failure and misfortune. Their passion and commitment towards the long-term objective helps give them the resilience needed to "stay the course" even when facing challenges and setbacks.

Psychologists define self-control as the ability to control and manage one's behavior, emotions and desires in order to obtain some reward. Self-control is essential for achievement as it keeps the person away from more impulsive tendencies that might not be in a person's best interest. Think of self-control as what one might need when on a diet. Walking by a patisserie, you may see a chocolate cake that looks extraordinarily delicious, but self-control keeps you from buying and eating the fattening temptation.

Grit theory supports the 10,000-hour rule developed by K. Anders Ericsson who stated that a successful person must perform or practice for 10,000 hours in order to be excellent. In *Outliers*, Malcolm Gladwell cites the Beatles' experience in Hamburg as their opportunity to practice as performers for an incredibly large amount of hours that led to their success.

What also must be added is that the Beatles while in Hamburg did not work or live in the best conditions. They had to perform in a very rough part of town known for prostitutes, gangsters and bar fights in front of tough audiences. All of them slept together in a small cinema's storeroom, which was cold, noisy, and next to the toilets. They had no hot water and washed up in the sink in the toilets. Still they did not quit and head back home to Liverpool; they persevered.

The Beatles had a long-term goal to be successful. Teenage John Lennon started a group with fellow teenagers Paul McCartney and George Harrison who all saw music as an escape from working class Liverpool. Their grit made them willing to work in appalling conditions in order to reach their long-term goal.

While grit is needed for success, self-control is also a prerequisite for the arduous road to success. A study of the daily schedule of classical violinists shows the importance of self-control. Elite violinists have a strict practice schedule that they follow each day while the middling classical violinists practice less and are more susceptible to having their attention diverted. Excellent violinists postpone personal pleasure for later, showing why self-control is important for success.

Both grit and self-control can be depleted as willpower can tire and people have only a certain reservoir of willpower. These days, self-control is even more difficult. The reason is not that we are weaker, but because society has created countless distractions around us to fill our immediate desires. As Kathleen Vohs, a University of Minnesota professor notes, "We are bombarded more and more with temptations," and "Our psychological systems is not set up to deal with all the potential immediate gratification."

Some social scientists have put forth the theory that people make a trade between self-control and grit. Some people use their willpower for grit by striving for long-term goals while others exercise self-control on a daily basis. Psychologists have recognized the need for grit and self-control in long-term goal setting, which is a key ingredient for accomplishment. Remember, success is not a sprint, but a marathon.

© David Baird

True Grit (Part 3)
Activity Sheet

True or False Quiz
Circle true or false based on the reading
1. Grit has only recently been heavily researched. — True/False
2. Self-control mainly manifests itself in long-term situations. — True/False
3. Angela Duckworth is a leading authority in the study of grit. — True/False
4. Self-control helps protect you from choosing things that might not be in your best interest. — True/False
5. To do well in your career, you need more grit than self-control. — True/False
6. The Beatles had an easy time when they worked in Hamburg. — True/False
7. Many people have an unlimited supply of willpower. — True/False
8. No one has any self-control anymore because there are too many temptations. — True/False
9. Sprinters need self-control while marathoners need grit. — True/False

Vocabulary Matching Quiz
A. Match the words on the left with the words with a similar meaning on the right

1. come to the fore　　　　a) diversions
2. perseverance　　　　　b) persist
3. stay the course　　　　c) thorough
4. setbacks　　　　　　　d) being visible
5. impulsive　　　　　　e) resolve
6. temptation　　　　　　f) overwhelmed
7. manifestation　　　　　g) rash
8. distractions　　　　　　h) indulgence
9. bombarded　　　　　　i) reversals
10. gratification　　　　　j) demonstration

B. Now, choose five of the words from the above vocabulary exercise and write five sentences below using each of those words in a sentence.
Example: I can't allow *setbacks* to discourage me.
a) _____
b) _____
c) _____
d) _____
e) _____

Classroom Discussion Questions
1. Do you have grit?
2. Have you ever given up something so you could be rewarded later?
3. Is it possible for someone to increase their willpower? How can someone increase their willpower?
4. Could you work in terrible conditions to become successful in the future? How long could you work in appalling conditions?
5. What temptation do you find difficult to deny yourself?
6. Who have you met that has very strong willpower? Why do you say so?
7. Do you think grit is important for someone to make significant accomplishments?
8. What are your long-term goals?

Write discussion questions for class discussions based on the topic in the article.
a) _____
b) _____
c) _____
d) _____
e) _____
f) _____

True Grit (Part 3) Lesson Notes

Today's Vocabulary

Words	Synonym	Antonym	Definition

Collocations/Phrases	Definition

What did I learn today?

What do I need to improve?

My homework for next class

Luck of the Draw (Part 4)

Warm Up

Classroom Discussion Questions
1. How do you define luck?
2. How has luck played a part in your life?
3. Complete the sentence - I'm lucky in _____ but unlucky in _____. Then explain your answer to your classmates.

Success and Failure Usage
Put the correct form of success or failure in the blanks in the sentences below. You may change the verb tense if needed.

| Success | Succeed | Successful | Successfully |
| Failure | Fail | Failing | Failed |

1. She _____ to get new clients so she closed her business.
2. The plan _____ because we all paid attention to details and we were well rehearsed.
3. We _____ completed the project on time and under budget.
4. His _____ was due to his hard work and a little luck.
5. Her personal _____ is telling people what to do, but never doing it herself.
6. My boss told me that _____ is not an option.
7. If you want to _____ in business, you must never quit and be ready to adapt.
8. Our presentation was very _____ as the client wants to talk to us next week.
9. We wish Kyle all the _____ in the world in his new job.
10. A few signs of a _____ business are high staff turnover, no new clients and heavy discounting.
11. Management has proudly stated that it has largely _____ in its aims.
12. A fear of _____ often deters people from trying something new.

Vocabulary Quiz

A. Choose words in each row that have a different meaning from the other words

1	lucky	golden	on a roll	cursed	fortunate
2	success	achievement	failure	accomplishment	triumph
3	influence	move	affect	dissuade	lead
4	bizarre	acceptable	strange	peculiar	odd
5	comprehensive	all-encompassing	vague	complete	widespread
6	second	era	time	period	age
7	misfortune	opening	break	opportunity	shot
8	adulation	adoration	praise	admiration	disrespect

B. Now, choose four of the words from the left column in the vocabulary exercise above and write four sentences below using each of those words in a sentence.
   a) _____
   b) _____
   c) _____
   d) _____

Comprehension Questions
Create three comprehension questions to quiz your classmates on how well they understand and remember the article.
Example: What business leaders are mentioned?
1. _____
2. _____
3. _____

Luck of the Draw

Success Is Not In Our Stars (Part 4)

So what makes someone successful? A high EQ, hard work and grit are definitely important, but two other factors that people are seldom aware of, but strongly influence their chances of success, are luck and looks. The problem is that people usually have little control over their own luck or looks.

Many people think luck is available for people who work hard, which is true. Bill Gates who considers himself a very fortunate man, was also successful because of his hard work put him in a position to have opportunities. However, luck comes in many forms. The first type of luck people have is the luck of birth. The luck of birth can be defined many ways. It could be which country you were born in, when you were born and whom your parents are, etc.

Which country you were born in can decide success or failure. An important need for success is education but in some countries, getting an education is difficult. If you are living in Bangladesh, the chances of being taught to read and write are a lot less than living in Japan. The literacy rate for Bangladesh is 56.8% (193rd in the world), while in Japan it is 99% (tied for 26th).

Your country of birth gives you a lot more opportunities than you might think. Other advantages of living in Japan are that it is a safe law-abiding society with comprehensive national health care and a developed economy that gives its people a high standard of living. All these things give you more favorable circumstances to be successful and increase your chances of leading a good life. Being born in Japan or countries such as the UK or Singapore gives you a better chance than the billions of people living in underdeveloped countries.

Demographics also plays a part with the luck of birth. People who are born in a year when the birth rate was low have a greater advantage than those who are born in a year with a high birth rate. When there are fewer people, then there is less competition to get accepted to good universities and to get choice jobs.

When you are born is also important. Certain eras have had more opportunity for people than others. Being born in the late 1830s in the USA was a great time (provided you were able to survive the American Civil War later in life) as some of the richest men in the history of the world were born during this time such as Andrew Carnegie, J.P. Morgan and John D. Rockefeller.

There is obviously the luck of whom your parents are. If your parents are rich that obviously gives you more advantages such as better education and social and business connections. Another advantage that many wealthy parents give their children is a sense of entitlement.

Entitlement is a sense of confidence that is quite helpful in being successful. It allows you to see people as your equals and not be intimidated by authority. Self-confidence is one of the keys to success as it allows you to not underestimate your value and your ideas' value. Confidence often attracts other people to follow you and makes you seen as a leader.

Given all the advantages that luck can bring to people it is sometimes bizarre to hear some very successful people describe themselves as self-made. Case in point is George W. Bush, who has described his success as self-made, yet his family connections allowed him to attend the two most prestigious universities in the US, Yale and Harvard while being a middling student. Family connections also benefited him throughout his business and political career.

Being a self-made success has a certain cachet as other supposed self-made successes have made the same absurd claims as Bush. While not belittling their success or hard work, their promotion of their self-made success stories often show that successful people start to delude themselves and do not see how fortune has smiled upon them.

© David Baird

Luck of the Draw (Part 4)
Activity Sheet

True or False Quiz
Based on the reading, choose whether the statements are true or false.
1. A high EQ, hard work, luck and looks are keys to success. — True/False
2. Bill Gates thinks he is a very lucky man. — True/False
3. Luck of birth is not very important. — True/False
4. Bangladesh people read more books than Japanese people do. — True/False
5. People born in the late 1820s in the USA became very rich. — True/False
6. When the birth rate is low, people have a better chance than those born in a year with a high birth rate. — True/False
7. Entitlement is a feeling of self-assurance. — True/False
8. Having rich parents is helpful to make people successful. — True/False
9. George W. Bush was not a self-made although he claimed he was. — True/False
10. Successful people want to be worshipped for their success. — True/False

Vocabulary Matching Quiz
A. Match the words on the left with the words with a similar meaning on the right

1. fortunate
2. literacy
3. law-abiding
4. underdeveloped
5. era
6. demographics
7. entitlement
8. intimidated
9. delude
10. belittling

a) population data
b) fool
c) frightened
d) lucky
e) period
f) Third World
g) ridicule
h) privilege
i) well-behaved
j) reading skills

B. Now, choose three of the words from the left column in the vocabulary exercise above and write three sentences below using each of those words in a sentence.
a) _____
b) _____
c) _____
d) _____

Classroom Discussion Questions
Write discussion questions based on the article. Next, ask your classmates your questions and make sure they give reasons.
a) _____
b) _____
c) _____
d) _____
e) _____
f) _____

Discuss the questions below with your classmates. Give reasons to your answers.
1. What advantages do you see living in your country?
2. What disadvantages do you see living in your country?
3. What disadvantages do you see women having in your country when trying to be successful?
4. When was the best time to be born in your country?
5. Can people with little self-confidence be successful?
6. Are there truly self-made successes?
7. Which successful person do you admire? Why?
8. Which successful person do you have little respect for? Why?

Luck of the Draw (Part 4) Lesson Notes

Today's Vocabulary

Words	Synonym	Antonym	Definition

Collocations/Phrases	Definition

What did I learn today?

What do I need to improve?

My homework for next class

Looks+Height=Success (Part 5)

Warm Up

Classroom Discussion Questions

1. Which short people do you admire?
2. Which tall people do you admire?
3. Whom would you like to look like?
4. Whom would you not like to look like?

Tall and Short Idioms

Below are some short and tall idioms marked in **bold**. After reading each sentence, write a definition for the idiom in the line below.

1. They've given us a **tall order** to complete the project in less than three weeks.

2. Intelligence, initiative and creativity are often in **short supply** at this company.

3. He told me a **tall tale** about having lunch with Norika Fujiwara.

4. I should go to the ATM now as I don't want to be **caught short** tonight.

5. He **stood tall** even though the team had lost the game.

6. That was a good wedding speech—**short and sweet**.

Looks Quotations

Put these quotations into your own words.

1. A clever, ugly man every now and then is successful with the ladies, but a handsome fool is irresistible.

2. Don't judge a book by its cover.

3. All that glitters is not gold.

4. Beauty is in the eye of the beholder.

5. Beauty is skin deep.

Reading Comprehension

Scan the article to find out the answers to the following questions.

a) What is a person called who is highly esteemed?
b) How many Fortune 500 CEOs were taller than 183 centimetres?
c) What is the importance of $789?
d) Which country has clinics to make children grow taller?
e) How much more money do good-looking people earn than average looking people?
f) What subject does Daniel Hamermesh teach?

Summarize the Article

After reading this article, please summarize this article in three sentences or less.

Looks+Height=Success

Success Is Not In Our Stars (Part 5)

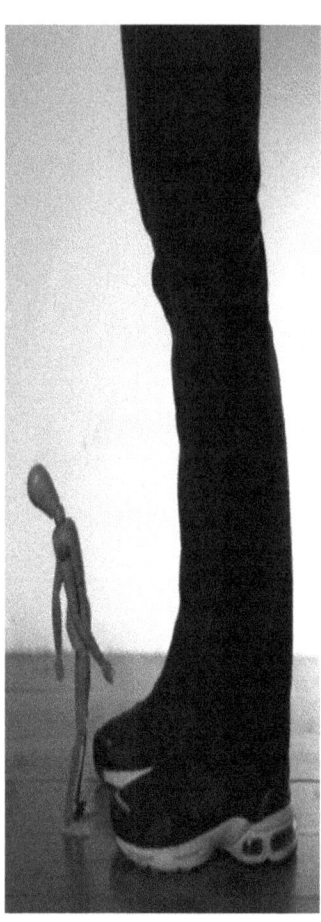

In the previous articles, emotional intelligence, grit, time and place of birth and hard work have been cited as keys to success. People have control over how much effort they make and emotional intelligence can be increased, but obviously not their birth.

One more factor that you have very little control over, which you receive from your parents is your looks. While people may not think that looks matter in this world, study after study show that looks have an important influence on helping people become successful.

The first physical advantage is height. This advantage shows up in the English language with metaphors for importance and power. When a person is highly esteemed, he is a "big man," and someone we "look up to" and we admire those who are "giants in their field." When we are confident, brave and self-assured, we "walk tall" Overall, height is admired and respected in the English culture.

However, it is not just in the English language that tall people are well regarded, but it also translates into work. Height has been shown to help in a person's success as taller people generally tend to be more successful than shorter people. It is not that taller people are smarter, more creative or better leaders, but people assume they have these talents especially as leaders. A 2004 survey of American Fortune 500 companies found that 58% of their CEOs were taller than 183 centimeters. For the US, the number of all people above 183 is 14%, so CEOs are outside the statistical norm.

Now looking over the general population, a 2004 survey by the University of Florida found that every 2.5 centimeters amounts to a salary increase of around $789 (¥60,061) per year. As people usually work around 40 years, the total salary difference over a career of someone being 170 to someone at 175 centimeters would be ¥4,804,080 over their career.

This trend is not just happening in the US and Europe, but has also been noticed in Asian countries. As the general population's height is getting taller in many Asian countries, being of greater stature is becoming more valuable than before. There are now clinics in South Korea giving treatments to help children become taller.

As for the value of good looks, University of California researchers found that attractive people made 12% more money than those regarded as plain looking. They found that beautiful people were wealthier and more successful, not just alluring. The study found that attractive people make more money because they find it easier to generate co-operation among their colleagues. Daniel Hamermesh, a University of Texas professor of economics, has researched this phenomenon and states that "Above-average-looking people were found to earn 5% more per hour than average-looking people." He also stated that, "It's pretty much universal across all occupations." Beauty may not only be skin deep, but it is often profitable as well.

Now at first, people may associate this trend as applying to women, but that is not the case. It applies as much to men as it does to women. There are many reasons that researchers have given for this trend. One reason is that good-looking people feel confident, so people are attracted to them.

Looks and height create powerful first impressions. While you cannot greatly change your looks and height unless you want to have plastic surgery, you can give the impression of confidence and reliability. A positive aura will diminish being judged by your looks. Good grooming, appropriate attire and cleanliness can also help beat the appearance phenomenon.

© David Baird

Looks+Height=Success (Part 5)
Activity Sheet

True or False Quiz
Based on the reading, choose whether the statements are true or false.

1. How good looking you are is an import factor in you being successful. True/False
2. Looking down on someone is an idiom meaning showing respect. True/False
3. Tall people are generally well-respected. True/False
4. American Fortune 500 company CEOs are, in general, taller than the average American. True/False
5. There are now clinics in Thailand giving treatments to help men become taller. True/False
6. Taller people make over ¥40 million more in their lifetime than shorter people. True/False
7. Good-looking people feel confident, so they demand to get higher salaries. True/False
8. No matter how self-assured and skilled you are, people will mainly judge you by your looks. True/False
9. Good grooming, appropriate attire and cleanliness can overcome the good-looks phenomenon. True/False

Vocabulary match
Match the words from the reading to synonyms on the left

1. matter   a) create
2. esteemed   b) tendency
3. generate   c) unattractive
4. trend   d) is significant
5. plain   e) reduce
6. alluring   f) widespread
7. universal   g) clothing
8. stature   h) respected
9. attire   i) appealing
10. diminish   j) build

Now choose five of the words on the left column and write five sentences below using each of those words in a sentence.

a) _____
b) _____
c) _____
d) _____
e) _____

Discussion Questions
Discuss the questions below with your classmates. Give your reasons.

1. Now that you have read this article, are you thinking of making any changes to your appearance?
2. How have your height and looks played a part in your life?
3. What height would you like to be?
4. Do you think good-looking people are more confident than average looking people?
5. Whom do you look up to?
6. When have you ever walked tall?
7. Do you think beauty is only skin-deep?
8. Can good grooming; appropriate attire and cleanliness help you be successful?

Write your discussion questions based on the article. Next, ask your classmates your questions and make sure they give reasons and details for their answers.

1. _____
2. _____
3. _____
4. _____

Looks+Height=Success (Part 5)
Lesson Notes

_____
_____
_____
_____
_____
_____
_____
_____
_____
_____
_____
_____

Today's Vocabulary

Words	Synonym	Antonym	Definition

Collocations/Phrases	Definition

What did I learn today?
_____
_____
_____

What do I need to improve?
_____
_____
_____

My homework for next class
_____
_____
_____

© David Baird

a) # Meeting Triumph and Disaster
Warm Up

Classroom Discussion Questions
1. Do you think the media covers business well?
2. What current CEOs do you admire? What current CEOs do you hold in low regard?

Vocabulary Finding Activity
A. Scan the article to find words that have similar meaning to the words below.
1) include _____
2) praise _____
3) reacting _____
4) critics _____
5) adeptly _____
6) danger signals _____
7) forethought _____
8) interruption _____
9) phonies _____
10) victory _____

B. Now, choose four of the words you found in the article and write four sentences below using each of those words in a sentence. You may change the word form.
a) _____
b) _____
c) _____
d) _____

Disaster and Triumph activity
Choose the correct word for each sentence from the four words below each line.
1. The flood was a _____ disaster.
   normal　　　　　　　natural　　　　　　　naturally　　　　　　　routine
2. Her election victory was hailed as a _____ triumph in the fight for women's equality.
   chief　　　　　　　key　　　　　　　minor　　　　　　　major
3. The company's poor cash flow was a _____ disaster.
   financial　　　　　　　corporation　　　　　　　finance　　　　　　　economics
4. The Fukushima nuclear accident was actually a(n) _____ disaster not a result of the tsunami.
   artificial　　　synthetic　　　　　　　unreal　　　　　　　man-made
5. A few market analysts _____ the disaster.
   predicted　　　　　　　guessed　　　　　　　presumed　　　　　　　supposed
6. Their recent triumph _____ the Giants surprised the odds makers.
   against　　　　　　　on　　　　　　　atop　　　　　　　above
7. She was confident that she would triumph _____ the competition.
   beside　　　　　　　over　　　　　　　atop　　　　　　　above

Summarize the Article
After reading this article, please summarize the article in three sentences or less.
_____
_____
_____
_____

Comprehension Questions
Create three comprehension questions to quiz your classmates on how well they understand and remember the article.
Example: What is the self-attributing bias?
a) _____
b) _____
c) _____

Meeting Triumph and Disaster

The CEO stands up at a press conference and pronounces that there will be a major change in the company. Possible scenarios could be an international expansion, acquisition of a well-known company, restructuring to cut costs. When the CEO makes the announcement, he or she will incorporate fashionable cutting edge ideas, popular business expressions and a catchy slogan.

The result after this announcement may even be a short-term bump in share price. Usually, the business media will applaud the CEO, especially those members of the media who want an interview. The reality on whether this new strategy is successful will only be seen in a few years, but optimism will be high weeks after the press conference.

If the strategy fails later, a little play will usually be performed for the public. In the first act, which is played out in the media, pundits will criticize the company's senior management for not having the proper foresight or lacking skill to competently execute their business strategy. The next act is usually the senior management responding by blaming external factors and circumstances that were beyond its control or impossible to foresee. The third act is usually a return to business as usual.

If you have a stake in that company, then warning bells should start to go off to distance yourself. According to the University of Iowa Business Professor Tyler Leverty, when a company goes under, it is more often not external factors, but the result of bad business decisions by the CEO.

All companies have to deal with outside forces that are beyond their control so blaming them is a bad excuse to hide behind. The reality of the situation is that the firm either did not plan well enough, foresee risks properly or had a structure unable to adapt to change. Failure and disruption happens to every company and how it deals with failure shows the executive team's true character. Executives, who cannot accept that their actions are the cause of failure, lack the ability to be self-critical. Self-criticism is essential in order to learn from mistakes, grow and gain an improved perspective.

Why do many business people lack the self-criticism and have a desire to be seen as infallible? One reason for this is a self-attributing bias. Self-attributing bias is a psychological term for believing you have the Midas touch when things go well and when something goes wrong, it is obviously someone else's fault. This bias has become even more prevalent today as many CEOs view themselves as movie stars or royalty deserving only praise. It would be better that CEOs heed Rudyard Kipling's adage that triumph and disaster are two imposters that should be treated just the same.

For a company to be sustainable, it must be filled with quality people starting at the top who can deal with unfavorable circumstances. Great management teams assume personal responsibility when things go bad and give credit to their employees when the business succeeds. Successful companies have these types of top-notch executive teams.

According to well-known psychologist Daniel Goleman, another reason high-ranking executives are less likely to have an accurate assessment of their individual performance is they often do not get the information they need to make informed decisions. Subordinates are often afraid to tell them the truth. Even when the boss tries to elicit contrary opinions, the boss may still give off negative signals such as a slight grimace or curt response, which transmits the message that bearing bad news is, in fact, uninvited

The worse part of all of this is when companies that play a significant role in the economy are led by terrible CEOs. One could look at the American banking industry or TEPCO, the Japanese utility company as examples. The senior management in these instances made serious errors of judgment yet their executives could not and still cannot accept responsibility that their management was the root of a major failure. Unluckily for all of us, their errors in judgment have caused major crises to occur.

© David Baird

Meeting Triumph and Disaster

Activity Sheet

True or False Quiz

Based on the reading, choose whether the statements are true or false.

1) The success of the latest business strategy can only be seen after a few years. True/False
2) Companies go bankrupt because of circumstances beyond their control. True/False
3) To succeed an organization should plan well, understand potential risks and be adaptable. True/False
4) Self-criticism is important so people can learn from mistakes and gain new insight. True/False
5) The self-attributing bias means you have the golden touch. True/False
6) All CEOs believe they should be treated as movie stars and never criticized. True/False
7) Rudyard Kipling stated that success and failure should be treated just the same. True/False
8) Usually executives indirectly discourage their staff from giving them accurate info. True/False
9) A good company must be filled with excellent people who can deal with unfavorable circumstances. True/False
10) A danger to society is that many critical companies are sometimes lead by terrible CEOs. True/False

Vocabulary Match

A. Match the words from the reading to synonyms or definitions on the left

1. pronounce
2. cutting edge
3. essential
4. infallible
5. bias
6. assessment
7. prevalent
8. Midas touch
9. elicit
10. grimace
11. curt

a) necessary
b) frown
c) evaluation
d) state
e) succeeds easily in business
f) common
g) abrupt
h) innovative
i) prejudice
j) ask for
k) perfect

B. Now, choose six of the words from the left column and write six sentences below using each word in a sentence.

a) _____
b) _____
c) _____
d) _____
e) _____
f) _____

Classroom Discussion Questions

Write your discussion questions based on the article. Next, ask your classmates your questions and make sure they give reasons and details for their answers.

1. _____
2. _____
3. _____
4. _____

Discuss the questions below with your classmates. Give your reasons.

1. Do you agree with the study that bad business decisions by the CEO cause most failures not external factors?
2. How should CEOs be evaluated? What should companies do when a CEO fails?
3. Have you ever been guilty of the self-attributing bias?
4. Are you good at evaluating your personal strengths and weaknesses?
5. What is more important for a company, an excellent executive team or a great CEO?

Meeting Triumph and Disaster
Lesson Notes

Today's Vocabulary

Words	Synonym	Antonym	Definition

Collocations/Phrases	Definition

What did I learn today?

What do I need to improve?

My homework for next class

Success Articles Vocabulary Review

Crossword Puzzle

Complete the crossword below with the clues given below. Some words are from articles from the preceding section. The letters in the squares are hints.

Across
1. Doorway, starting point
5. Cutting _____
7. Lemon taste
9. Unfavorable, unlucky
12. Be full of, be overflowing
14. Stretch
15. Peers
17. A holy person
19. Limit, stop
20. Gershwin or Glass
22. An historic age
23. Frowned
24. Inquire, pose
25. New Year's _____ Party

Down
1. Don't rush
2. You need one to listen
3. Pay attention
4. Let's _____ for today
5. Necessary
6. _____ income
8. Safe
10. Travel through
11. Salmon eggs
13. Draws out
16. Clothes
17. What Thailand was once called
18. Swap, buy and sell
20. Drink cooler
21. Accelerate, speed up

Fill in the Blank Activity

Fill in the blanks in the sentences below with the words in the box. You may have to change the word form in the sentence.

| counterintuitive | perseverance | deal with | adapt |
| perceive | continual | take the time | setbacks |

1. The Earth being round and orbiting the sun is _____ to our observations.
2. We seldom _____ to stop and smell the roses in our busy schedule.
3. What people _____ to be true and what is true is sometimes quite different.
4. He needs to _____ his own problems, before he can do anything else.
5. She has quickly _____ to living in Thailand.
6. There have been _____ fights between marketing and production on why the last few product rollouts failed.
7. His _____ is why he has succeeded against incredible odds.
8. Despite some early _____ the product y eventually became a market leader.

Success Articles Vocabulary Review

Success Stories

Warren Buffet

Put the following words into the spaces below.

    elite   continued   peers.   taking the time
    trends   esteems   plain   cutting edge
    Midas touch   cornerstone   infallible

    When it comes to making money, few come close to Warren Buffet, the CEO of and largest shareholder of Berkshire Hathaway, one of the world's most respected companies. In the world of _____ investors, he has no _____.

    Buffet, nicknamed the Oracle of Omaha, seems to have the _____, as Berkshire Hathaway seems to go from one success to another. It has 18.3% annualized returns in Berkshire Hathaway's book value over the past 30 years. However, he is not _____ as he has made poor decisions when buying textile and oil companies and predicting the recovery of the US housing market in 2011.

    What also sets Buffet apart from other captains of industry is that Buffet is known for his _____-spoken style which _____ him in many eyes. He generates quotes that are direct and to the point such as "If you get into a lousy business, get out of it," and "If you want to be known as a good manager, buy a good business." In addition, he is not one to promote _____technology or the latest _____. He is a good friend of Bill Gates, yet he professes no idea on how IT companies make their money.

    The _____ to his _____ success is he believes in investing in companies then _____ to see them increase in value. He is interested in the long term not the short-term return. Additionally, Buffet does not believe in investing in a company whose business model he does not understand.

Early Retirement

Put the following words into the spaces below.

    perceive   alluring   fortunate   deliberate
    material   asserted   exhaustive   prevalent
    world-renowned   diminishing   deal with
    continual   literary   self-assessment   entitled

    In our culture where _____ success has become the _____ mantra, there are anomalies, people who are at the top of their careers suddenly walking away and never returning. There was the _____Swedish actress Greta Garbo who left Hollywood at the peak of her fame and _____ all she wanted was to be left alone. Another dropout was the writer J.D. Salinger who at the height of his _____ career left to live in a small town in New Hampshire.

    It is strange for many of us to _____ that someone so great would suddenly walk away from fame and fortune. The adulation, fame and money most people would find _____yet for them and others it was not. What makes these _____ few make a strange but _____choice to retire early?

    While there have been _____ studies on why people are successful, there are very few studies on why people would quit. It is essential for us to note that the reasons for early retirement vary from person to person. For athletes and some performers they see their skills _____ and no longer want to _____life on the road and the _____ practicing.

    For others, they believe they have nothing more to offer. They have gone through some _____ and realized they have done everything they wanted to do. Whatever their reason, they are _____ to retire and if people are fans they should thank them for what they have done.

© David Baird

Word Form Activity

Complete the table with the words from the articles by writing their related forms in the appropriate columns.

Verb	Noun	Adjective
pronounce		xxxxxxxxx
xxxxxxxxx		essential
adapt		
delude		
	assessment	xxxxxxxxx
	perseverance	
perceive		
	distraction	
		energetic
think		
		tolerant
	gratification	
deliberate		
exhaust		

Now, choose seven of the words from above and write seven sentences below using each word in a sentence.

a) _____
b) _____
c) _____
d) _____
e) _____
f) _____
g) _____

Collocation Activity

Collocations are the usual matching or combining of a particular word with another word or words that are commonly used together in English. Think of collocations as words that usually go together.

Circle the correct word in each of the 12 sentences to make the collocation.

1. We need to *locally/regionally* generate revenue.
2. We have now tried to *correct/remedy* the bias in our original report
3. Young people are usually more *computer/digital* literate than older people are.
4. I *avoid/evade* temptation to drink by staying away from bars.
5. We *calculate/count* ourselves extremely fortunate.
6. His research has *suffered from/been ill with* a temporary setback.
7. Excessive exposure to sunlight speeds up the *ageing/maturing* process of the skin.
8. He showed *large/great* perseverance by staying in the job.
9. He's very perceptive *about/of* people.
10. It is *coming/becoming* almost essential for students to speak a second language.
11. The country has *come into/entered* an era of high unemployment.
12. She has an extremely low *pain/agony* threshold.

Writing Activity

In 150 words or more, what advice would you give to someone who wants to be successful?

_____
_____
_____
_____
_____
_____
_____
_____
_____
_____
_____
_____
_____

Management Discussion Articles

Organic vs. Non-Organic
Warm Up

Article Prediction
Before reading the article, what do you think the article is about?
_____
_____

Classroom Discussion Activity
1. Do you know any examples of a successful merger or acquisition?
2. Do you know any examples of a failed merger or acquisition?

Vocabulary Finding Activity
A. Find words in the article that mean
1. fruits and vegetables _____
2. great quantity _____
3. kingdom _____
4. huge _____
5. complication _____
6. worried _____
7. originality _____
8. call _____
9. is likely to _____
10. all-inclusive _____
11. assimilation _____
12. meticulously _____

B. Now, choose six of the words you found in the article in Activity A and write six sentences below. You may change the form of the words.
a) _____
b) _____
c) _____
d) _____
e) _____
f) _____

Reading Comprehension
After reading the article, answer the following questions.

1. What seven qualities does the author cite as needed for organic growth?
   _____
2. What is the difference between a merger and an acquisition?
   _____
3. What are good reasons for an acquisition?
   _____
4. Name an obstacle that may cause an acquisition to fail?
   _____
5. Which companies are successful in acquiring companies?
   _____

Article Summary
Summarize the article in three sentences or less.
_____
_____
_____
_____
_____

Comprehension Questions
Create three comprehension questions to quiz your classmates on how well they understand and remember the article.
Example: What is the success rate of acquisitions?
1. _____
2. _____
3. _____

Not to be copy or reproduced in any form unless granted permission

Organic vs. Non-Organic

When business people talk about organic growth, they are usually not talking about organic food or a new organic produce section in the supermarket but rather a business expansion to increase its customer base. However, organic growth and growing organic food are similar in one aspect they are both difficult to do.

For a company to grow organically after it matures, it must create a successful new product, open new markets, and develop a long-term sustainable growth strategy. All of that requires creativity, innovation and skill along with some money, luck, intelligence and time. These qualities are rarely in abundance. So many companies choose instead the non-organic method instead, mergers and acquisitions (M&As). If you cannot build it or make it, then buy it.

First, what is a merger and acquisition? A merger is when two companies come together as equals. Acquisitions are when one company buys another company. Mergers are rarer than acquisitions. However, many CEOs often label acquisitions as mergers to give the illusion that the purchased company and its employees are equal partners.

Good reasons for companies to choose the M&A route is to strengthen their business by filling gaps in their product range, increasing skill sets and services, and getting content. Additionally a company could also want to gain access to new customers and markets and try to improve economies of scale.

On the other hand, many companies make acquisitions for the wrong reasons. They buy because every other company is doing it, or upper management wants to build an empire. Additionally they want to add revenue regardless of whether the newly purchased company fits their company's business strategy or not. These are bad reasons for making acquisitions as it makes companies more prone to failure than success.

Acquisition failure according to some studies is somewhere between 70 to 90% and companies spend around two trillion dollars a year in M&A deals. Why is the failure rate so high, given that the amount of money is so immense? As mentioned previously, bad reasons for purchasing are an important factor for acquisition failure, as well as making errors during the deal-making process and finally managing the post-acquisition integration phase poorly.

After that, the biggest problem in the deal-making process is that the buyer pays too much. Overpayment can result in buyers having to sell off assets or make damaging personnel cuts. The outcome then is the business going into decline.

Managing the post-deal phase is the next obstacle to overcome as failure is often caused by poor integration. For instance, many buyers do not usually have a comprehensive integration plan on how to handle the post-acquisition process. As well, they have not thoroughly examined the newly acquired company's business model and culture. Additionally the acquirer poorly communicates his goals to the new and anxious employees.

So given all the obstacles that need to be overcome, how can a company successfully acquire another? First, look at the companies that are successful at acquisitions such as Japan Tobacco, Cisco and General Electric. Their acquisition targets fit their business model and they accurately appraise its value, and finally, they have a concrete integration plan. If a firm can understand these three points, the acquisition will be successful for the buyer and not just for the investment banker who arranged the deal.

© David Baird

Organic vs. Non-Organic Activity Sheet

True or False Quiz

According to the reading, circle whether the statements below are true or false

1.	Most business people are concerned about how to grow organic food.	True/False
2.	Money, luck, intelligence and time are needed for a company to expand.	True/False
3.	CEOs often call acquisitions mergers so the acquired company employees do not see themselves as losers.	True/False
4.	A good reason for an M&A is your investment banker recommended it.	True/False
5.	Companies may want to improve their economies of scale by buying a competitor.	True/False
6.	Companies make acquisitions to follow what their competitors are doing.	True/False
7.	Acquisition success is somewhere between 20 to 40%.	True/False
8.	Paying too much for a new acquisition will not harm the company in the short term.	True/False
9.	Most executives have a fully thought out plan on how to manage the post-acquisition integration process.	True/False
10.	Companies should study JT, Cisco and GE so they can be successful at executing M&As.	True/False

Vocabulary Activity

A. Complete the sentences with grammatically correct forms of the words from the reading.

examine   prone   access   illusion   abundance

1. My co-worker is _____ to forget his wallet when he is drinking.
2. Some people are under the _____ that he is kind, but that would be wrong.
3. There is an _____ of polite people in Japan.
4. Only a few people have _____ to the research and development labs.
5. A good critical thinker _____ a problem from all sides.

Discussion Activity

Please discuss the questions below with your classmates. Ask your classmates follow-up questions if needed. In addition, give detailed reasons for your answers.

1. Has your company mainly grown organically or by M&As? Has the strategy been successful?
2. In your industry, how do most companies expand, organically or by M&As? Which strategy do you think is best?
3. If you were the CEO, how would you grow your company?
4. If your company was acquired, how would you feel? Would you stay?
5. How would you like the new employer to treat you? What should they tell you?
6. What should new employers tell employees of newly acquired companies?
7. What other reasons are there for companies to make acquisitions?
8. Given that most acquisitions do not succeed, why do companies keep on acquiring?
9. In spite of the evidence of so many failures, why do companies keep on failing when they buy a new company?
10. If you were in charge of the integration process, what would you tell the new employees?

Additional Questions for Discussion

Write discussion questions for class discussions based on the topic in the article. Next, ask your classmates your questions and make sure they give reasons.

a) _____
b) _____
c) _____
d) _____
e) _____

Organic vs. Non-Organic Lesson Notes

_____
_____
_____
_____
_____
_____
_____
_____
_____
_____
_____
_____

Today's Vocabulary

Words	Synonym	Antonym	Definition

Collocations/Phrases	Definition

What did I learn today?
_____
_____
_____

What do I need to improve?
_____
_____
_____

My homework for next class
_____
_____
_____

The Importance of Questions

Warm Up

Classroom Discussion Questions
1. Can you give an example of when you have asked a stupid question?
2. Can you give an example of when you have been asked a stupid question?

What is the question? Activity
Below are answers to various questions but what are the questions? Write the questions on the line above each answer.

1. _____
   It's ¥385 yen less per unit than the competition and is more reliable.
2. _____
   I'm sorry, we only ship to the US and Canada.
3. _____
   The document should be a PDF.
4. _____
   Our first step is to define our project goal and then to collect all relevant materials such as contracts, organizational processes, etc.
5. _____
   Organic growth is expanding your business by increasing your overall customer base.
6. _____
   We should definitely consider using freelancers to keep costs down.
7. _____
   Generally, I advocate moving brick and mortar businesses to go online, but there are certain industries that shouldn't.

What Should You Ask? Activity
In the following situations, what questions need to be asked? Write down all questions that you can think of for each particular situation below that need to be raised.

1) You are at a meeting with members of the HR team to discuss a troublesome salesperson, Andrea Lindsay. She is the top salesperson but has caused considerable problems in the sales team, as she is often uncooperative. She does not often come to meetings and her paperwork is sometimes incomplete. She is also not very positive and is critical of her coworkers. However, she is the best closer on the sales team and her customers love her.

   _____
   _____
   _____
   _____
   _____
   _____
   _____
   _____
   _____
   _____

2) You have a visitor coming from South Korea who is looking to start a new alliance with you. It could mean a five-year deal of over 15 billion yen with a 10% return for your company. You are now in a meeting with members of your team to decide how to entertain her and what your strategy will be when you start your first formal meeting.

   _____
   _____
   _____
   _____
   _____
   _____
   _____
   _____
   _____
   _____

The Importance of Questions

"There are no stupid questions, only stupid answers," which means that it is okay to ask any question. It is the responder's reply to a question that can show their stupidity or their lack of manners.

Usually this maxim is true, but there are exceptions. Questions are deemed stupid if they are irrelevant, ask something obvious, or are out of left field. In addition, if the question has been asked and answered a few times already, or if it is considered rude, if too personal, too blunt or too aggressive. People often take offense to these types of questions, so the answer you may receive may be neither stupid nor polite. However, remember that what seems like a stupid question to one person, might be a key question for someone else, and could raise an important point.

Overall questions are important for companies as they can stop "groupthink" which can make organizations complacent, arrogant and reduce creativity. What is groupthink? Groupthink was first defined by psychologist Irving Janis as a group making faulty decisions because of pressures to conform to the group's values or ethics.

More often groupthink is used to describe when all people in a particular group are thinking similarly, and so do not question actions or decisions. While some social scientists argue that groupthink has some positive aspects such as quicker decisions and improving efficiency, most people see it as negative. It does reduce conflict but alternative ideas are not considered. With this mindset, people inside the group very rarely oppose each other's point of view or way of thinking. In some large organizations and industrial sectors, groupthink has been a problem.

Groupthink can cause people to overestimate their collective power and infallibility, often causing the group to be close-minded, filter out contradictory information and overemphasize uniformity. Other dangers that Irving Janis, a noted Yale psychologist, identified from groupthink were groups possessing excessive optimism that encourages taking tremendous risks; ignoring the ethical or moral consequences of their decisions; and creating the illusion that all views and judgments are unanimous.

A good example of groupthink is the US financial industry over the last 15 years. As profits and bonuses rose dramatically due to the banks overleveraging and selling convoluted financial instruments, some notable people, both from inside and outside the industry, proclaimed that many banks were carrying too much risk. Furthermore, many members of the establishments did not fully understand the financial instruments. These independent thinkers were swiftly and roundly criticized, ignored or ostracized.

How strong is groupthink? Even after the crash of 2008, many of the ideas and ways of thinking, which caused the disaster, persist in the financial industry. Groupthink ideas can be like an enduring movie monster that rarely dies.

Some companies have an in-house "*devil's advocate*" so they can fight against groupthink becoming entrenched within a company. The devil's advocate (the devil's lawyer) job is to take the opposing side of an issue and search for faults. Finding faults before a proposal becomes a reality may save the company money and its reputation.

Now most companies do not have a position called the devil's advocate, but instead they have a risk manager. Risk managers identify, assess, and prioritize risks and then advise organizations on how potential risks could affect the profitability or existence of the company. They will also suggest a course of action to hedge or counteract the threat.

While devil's advocates are very important, they are rarely appreciated as they are often seen as being over cautious and an obstacle to earning profits and staff receiving bonuses. However without decision makers willing to listen to the existence of potential trouble, companies may sink. Just ask AIG, TEPCO, and Merrill Lynch whether they could have handled risk better.

© David Baird

The Importance of Questions

Activity Sheet

True or False Quiz

Circle whether the statement is true or false based on the reading.

1. There are no stupid answers, only stupid questions. — True/False
2. Questions may be seen as foolish if they ask the obvious. — True/False
3. Groupthink is defined as the act of a group making a decision. — True/False
4. The positive aspects of groupthink are quick decisions and efficiency. — True/False
5. Groupthink may cause management to believe they never make a mistake. — True/False
6. Criticism of the banking industry before 2008 was well received. — True/False
7. Groupthink ideas are monsters that attacked Tokyo. — True/False
8. Devil's advocates usually argue in support of popular ideas. — True/False
9. AIG, Countrywide, and Merrill Lynch should have had more people in the organization questioning their operations. — True/False

Vocabulary Matching Activity

A. Match the words on the left with their definitions on the right

1. out of left field
2. complacency
3. infallibility
4. ostracizd
5. convoluted
6. uniformity
7. persist
8. entrench
9. reputation

a) to strongly establish or embed
b) status, character, standing
c) too complex so it can not be understood
d) standardization, sameness
e) never wrong, perfect
f) wildly unrelated to the subject being discussed
g) unaware or uninformed self-satisfaction
h) to be ignored or expelled from a social group
i) endure, live on, continue

B. Now, choose five of the words from the left column above and write five sentences below using each word in a different sentence.

a) _____
b) _____
c) _____
d) _____
e) _____

Discussion Questions

Write questions for class discussions based on the topic in the article. Next, ask your classmates your questions and make sure they give reasons. Ask follow-up questions if necessary.

a) _____
b) _____
c) _____
d) _____
e) _____

Please discuss the questions below with your classmates. Ask your classmates follow _up questions if needed. In addition, give detailed reasons to your answers.

1. How would you describe your questioning style? Friendly and open or to the point and direct?
2. What is groupthink? Can you give an example?
3. Do you think groupthink is good or bad?
4. Does your organization ever suffer from groupthink?
5. Does your society do a good job of questioning its leaders?
6. Do you ever argue against popular opinions?
7. How do you feel when your actions are questioned?
8. If you were a risk manager for your company, what would you worry about?

The Importance of Questions Lesson Notes

_____
_____
_____
_____
_____
_____
_____
_____
_____
_____

Today's Vocabulary

Words	Synonym	Antonym	Definition

Collocations/Phrases	Definition

What did I learn today?
_____
_____
_____

What do I need to improve?
_____
_____
_____

My homework for next class
_____
_____
_____

A Delicate Balance

Warm Up

Idiom Definitions

Read the sentences below and then match the definition with the idioms that are in bold.

1. The partnership between politicians and civil servants is **a delicate balance** as politicians have one view on what should be done and civil servants have a differing view of what can be done.
2. Norwegian research scientists have found that there **is a thin line between** genius and insanity as they both share the same genes.
3. We must all **strike a balance between** what we want and what we need to do.
4. Science is **a double-edged sword** as it can cure disease but also produces nuclear bombs.
5. I've been **walking a tightrope** for the last three months as my biggest customer left and we have a lot of bills to pay.
6. He is **sitting on the fence**, not saying yes or no.

1. A delicate balance
2. A thin line between
3. Strike a balance
4. Double-edged sword
5. Walking a tightrope
6. Sitting on the fence

a) Two concepts seeming to be different yet very close. The second one is usually bad
b) To be in a situation where one must be very cautious
c) Hesitance to choose between two opposing
d) Something that can both help and harm
e) To find a satisfactory compromise between two extremes
f) Something that can easily tip either way

Now choose two of the idioms in the activity above and write two sentences in the lines below

a) _____
_____
b) _____
_____

Classroom Discussion Questions

1. Can you give an example of a delicate balance?
2. What do you find difficult to strike a balance between?
3. Is there a thin line between love and hate?

Vocabulary Finding Activity

A. Find words in the article that have a similar meaning to the following words

1) anarchy _____
2) vibrant _____
3) negligence _____
4) supervision _____
5) inclinations _____
6) obstruct _____
7) narrow-minded _____
8) implement _____
9) review _____
10) structure _____
11) guarantee _____
12) calamity _____

B. Now, choose seven of the words you found in the article in Activity A and write seven sentences below

a) _____
b) _____
c) _____
d) _____
e) _____
f) _____
g) _____

A Delicate Balance

Almost all activities need some basic rules from simple children's games like tag to the running of a national government. As societies develop complex organizations, they require organizers and administrators to administer the rules. Without rules, chaos, confusion and corruption would reign.

Nevertheless, how many rules and regulations does society need for it to function? When are there too many or too few rules? To find that delicate balance which allows an institution to still be dynamic, creative and flexible while not failing due to a lack of discipline and mismanagement is a challenge.

Ardent capitalists will argue that there should be little or no rules in markets as an invisible hand rules them. The invisible hand is supposed to efficiently allocate goods and services in all markets. However, the 1929 Stock Market Crash and the 2008 Financial Crisis show how that argument endangers the well-being of society as markets unrestrained by oversight and regulation will crash. As those two historical events demonstrate, rules are essential in order to protect society from the financial industry's self-destructive tendencies.

Conversely, too much regulation can hinder progress by bogging people down who have to follow Byzantine procedures, fill out countless amounts of convoluted forms and then wait for approval from nameless administrators. This process is called red tape. For the people desiring action or progress, red tape becomes an annoying, frustrating, barrier to excellence.

Red tape and the petty bureaucrats who administer and enforce it are often associated with governments, but it is not just governments where bureaucracy can be found as large corporations can fall victim to the malaise of red tape. Of course, some form of bureaucracy is essential, because of a company's size. Additionally some industries are subject to serious regulatory scrutiny, since the lack of oversight could have catastrophic consequences.

An organization still faces the conundrum of designing rules to remain flexible and adaptable. To overcome that dilemma, well-known business consultant and writer Jim Collins has stated that a company needs to hire disciplined people who understand the core values of the organization. Additionally the cornerstone of the company's culture should be that within a certain framework there should be freedom and responsibility. So long as people stay within the bounds of the framework, they should have freedom to innovate, achieve and contribute. Collins seesthat the purpose of bureaucracy is to keep incompetence and lack of discipline in check.

Of course, with Collins' philosophy there is one major problem; a corporation has to ensure that they hire disciplined people. When a corporation increases in size, it automatically faces the growing risk that it may hire someone who does not adhere to its core values, or is mediocre or inept. An incompetent employee who slips through the cracks in the hiring process can be dangerous. That one employee's misstep, especially when that employee is in a key position, can lead to a catastrophe.

A serious employee blunder demonstrates why hiring should be rigorous; compensation has to be above the average and new employee training should be exemplary. Otherwise, the company will have to create numerous rules and regulations to protect itself from its own inept hires.

© David Baird

A Delicate Balance Activity Sheet

True or False Quiz
According to the reading, circle whether the statements below are true or false
1. When societies mature, they required managers and bureaucrats. — True/False
2. It is easy for companies to be disciplined and well-managed while still being dynamic, creative and flexible. — True/False
3. Some plutocrats believe in free markets. — True/False
4. Many rules can contribute to the progress and action of a company. — True/False
5. The 2008 financial crisis showed the importance of internal oversight control. — True/False
6. An organization has to tackle the problem of designing regulations while still remaining flexible and rigid. — True/False
7. Business consultant Jim Collins stated that a company should employ people who are disciplined and understand the company's principles. — True/False
8. One bad employee can never harm a company. — True/False
9. Disciplined employees can be given a lot of freedom provided they stay within a framework. — True/False
10. Companies may need red tape to protect themselves from their own bad employees. — True/False

Vocabulary Matching Activity
A. Match the words from the reading to synonyms or definitions on the left.

1. corruption   a) excellent
2. reign   b) error
3. delicate   c) rule
4. ardent   d) passionate
5. Byzantine   e) bungling
6. malaise   f) overly complex
7. exemplary   g) illness
8. keep in check   h) dishonesty
9. inept   i) control
10. blunder   j) fragile

B. Now, choose five of the words from the left side above and write five sentences below using each word in a different sentence.
a) _____
b) _____
c) _____
d) _____
e) _____

Classroom Discussion Questions
Write questions for class discussions based on the topic in the article. Next, ask your classmates your questions and make sure they give reasons. Ask follow-up questions if necessary.
a) _____
b) _____
c) _____
d) _____

Please discuss the questions below with your classmates. Ask your classmates follow-up questions if needed. In addition, give detailed reasons to your answers.
1. Does your organization have too many rules?
2. What rules would you like to change in your organization?
3. Do you think people forget why rules exist? Why or why not?
4. Do you agree with Jim Collins that the purpose of bureaucracy is to compensate for incompetence and lack of discipline?
5. A commentator recently stated that Japanese have perfected bureaucracy. What do you think he meant?
6. Would you describe your organization's hiring process as rigorous?
7. How can a company make sure it does not have too much red tape?

Delicate Balance Lesson Notes

Today's Vocabulary

Words	Synonym	Antonym	Definition

Collocations/Phrases	Definition

What did I learn today?

What do I need to improve?

My homework for next class

The Buck No Longer Stops Anywhere
Warm Up

Article Prediction
Before reading the article, read the phrases below, which are from the article. After reading the phrases, write down your prediction of what the article is about.
- accepted responsibility for his own actions
- consultants strongly advise leaders to avoid publicity
- choose to avoid, evade and duck the question
- functions and products not shared within a company
- promotes a taking responsibility culture within the entire company

_____
_____

Classroom Discussion Questions
1. What corporate scandal can you recall? Why was it damaging? Did it harm the company in the long run?
2. When a famous person publicly avoids, evades or ducks the question, what do you think of them?

Vocabulary Activity
Circle the word in each row that does not belong with the others

Lie	Half Truth	Fib	Misstatement	Fact
Candor	Honesty	Duplicity	Frankness	Openness
Evade	Face	Duck	Skirt	Avoid
Dishonest	False	Sincere	Cunning	Deceitful
Be Straight	Mislead	Bluff	Distort	Lie
Explain	Clarify	Disclose	Hide	Make Plain
Vague	Ambiguous	Confusing	Clear	Hazy
Proceed	Delay	Put off	Stall	Defer
Back pedal	Answer	Dodge	Steer clear of	Sidestep

Good Excuse/Bad Excuse
After reading the article, mark beside each of these well-known excuses either **G** for good excuse and **B** for bad excuse. Afterwards with another classmate go over your answers and explain your choices.

- It's not my department.
- I won't do it because I don't want other people in my section to look bad.
- I won't be in today. I'm still drunk from last night.
- I'm not the most qualified person for the job.
- Homework? I don't remember getting any homework?
- I know I made a mistake, but I think you're overlooking all the times I've done a good job.
- Some things have come up and need my attention.
- I'm sorry, did you mean that you wanted that done right now?
- I hate to split my time between so many projects.
- I'm sorry, but I've been working quite hard so I need to recharge my batteries.
- I didn't do it because I don't understand what my boss really wants.

Comprehension Questions
Create four comprehension questions to quiz your classmates on how well they understand and remember the article.
Example: Who is Alan Greenspan?

a) _____
b) _____
c) _____
d) _____

The Buck No Longer Stops Anywhere

Harry S Truman, the 33rd president of the US, kept a sign in the Oval Office saying, "The buck stops here." What this saying means is that he accepted responsibility for his actions and the actions of people who report to him.

This simple expression has become a popular way to express accountability. Accountability is acknowledging and assuming responsibility for any actions, decisions and policies made while someone is the leader of a particular organization. Included in the scope of accountability is also an obligation to report, explain and answer for any consequences caused by the organization's actions.

When people do not accept responsibility, we say they are "passing the buck." When someone passes the buck, they are avoiding responsibility for any action or incident and giving the responsibility to someone else. Almost all crisis management consultants strongly advise leaders to avoid publicly shifting the blame as it is considered a sign of weak leadership. Yet it persists. Why it continues to happen after numerous embarrassing corporate incidents showing the negative effects of not making a public apology is still a mystery.

One reason could be that some people in positions of prominence choose to avoid, evade and duck questions. Many fear a direct answer or an admission of responsibility will hurt their image, contradict their personal beliefs or even worse threaten their job.

A case in point is Alan Greenspan, the former Federal Reserve Chairman who was questioned about his role in causing the 2008 Financial Crisis. Before the crisis, Greenspan, who was against almost all market regulations, was revered by many as the maestro who skillfully managed the US monetary supply, which helped ensure America's economic growth. Greenspan throughout his career had argued against regulation, as he believed that the free market was self-correcting and would rectify any flaws.

In October 2008, before a Congressional committee, Greenspan appeared to explain his actions. At that time, Greenspan was retired, so he did not have to worry about his job, but he was worried about his legacy and his beliefs were in question. Greenspan could only admit that he was "partially" wrong in opposing regulation. This explanation stated that the US financial industry, which Greenspan oversaw, had led the economy to collapse to levels not seen since 1929 and the Great Depression.

Organizations can also have a pass the buck mentality. Organizations have many built in excuses — information, functions and products not shared within the company, poor communication, undefined chain of command, uneven budget allocations, and legacy issues. This way of thinking can result in product failures, supply chain disruptions, fraud, missed sales forecasts and more. Sometimes the results can be catastrophic such as the BP Horizon oil spill or TEPCO's handling of the Fukushima nuclear problem.

To prevent such problems an organization's senior management has to create a set of principles, which will establish proper conduct and promote a culture of people taking responsibility within the entire company. In addition, middle managers must feel comfortable in assessing and managing risk, and in making sure that front-line employees understand risk management.

Focusing on individuals to take responsibility will strengthen people to find ways to prevent problems. Stopping buck-passing can be a method for saving human lives, protecting an organization's integrity and in business and increasing profitability.

© David Baird

The Buck No Longer Stops Anywhere Activity Sheet

True or False Quiz
Circle True or False based on the reading.
1. Accountability is something that CPAs and CGAs learn. — True/False
2. Harry S Truman, 33rd president of the US, kept a sign in the Oval Office saying "The buck stops somewhere." — True/False
3. Alan Greenspan was a big believer in financial regulations. — True/False
4. Powerful people may avoid responsibility because they do not want to look bad. — True/False
5. Almost all crisis management consultants counsel leaders not to clearly answer questions. — True/False
6. Company personnel have many excuses for passing the buck such as poor communication, no clear leadership and legacy issues. — True/False
7. TEPCO is a good example of a company that practices accountability. — True/False
8. To prevent passing the buck, an organization should have staff create a set of guidelines so that everyone behaves. — True/False

Vocabulary Matching Activity
A. Match the words from the reading on the left with similar meaning words on the right.

1. accountability
2. scope
3. prominence
4. revered
5. maestro
6. flaw
7. legacy
8. mentality
9. allocations
10. disruption

a) genius
b) attitude
c) importance
d) area
e) answerability
f) honored
g) symbol of his work
h) distributions
i) commotion
j) fault

B. Now, choose four of the words on the left side from the above vocabulary exercise and write four sentences below using each of those words in a sentence. You may change the form of the words.

a) _____
b) _____
c) _____
d) _____

Classroom Discussion Questions
Discuss the questions below with your classmates. Give your reasons.
1. Do you *pass the buck* or does the *buck stop here* when something goes wrong?
2. How can someone be partially wrong?
3. Which is your organization's biggest problem: functions and products not shared within, poor communication, undefined chain of command, uneven budget allocations, or legacy issues?
4. Of the problems above which is the hardest to fix? How would you fix it?
5. What advice would you give a CEO if his company was involved in a scandal?

Additional Questions for Discussion
Write questions for class discussions based on the topic in the article. Next, ask your classmates your questions and make sure they give reasons. Ask follow up-questions if necessary.

a) _____
b) _____
c) _____
d) _____
e) _____

The Buck No Longer Stops Here Lesson Notes

_____
_____
_____
_____
_____
_____
_____
_____

Today's Vocabulary

Words	Synonym	Antonym	Definition

Collocations/Phrases	Definition

What did I learn today?
_____
_____
_____
_____

What do I need to improve?
_____
_____
_____
_____

My Homework for Next Class
_____
_____

Management Articles Vocabulary Review

Fill in the Blank Activity

A. Fill in the blanks in the sentences below with the words in the box. You may have to change the word form in the sentence.

catastrophe	infallible	complacent	blunder	chaos
mismanagement		go under	employee	

A: I tell you it's _____ over at Beta Systems. After years of _____, the company is going to go under.
B: How bad is it?
A: Terrible! Well, besides the company _____ and 856 people going to lose their jobs there are also 15 to 24 suppliers who will go _____ within the year.
C: How did it happen?
A: Management thought they were _____ and they wouldn't listen to anyone. They kept on thinking that the markets and their customers had not changed.
B: You mean they became _____?
A: Yup, by the time they realized that things had changed, it was too late. Even then, they kept on _____ and went from one _____ to the next.
C: What next?
A: Well unless, they get a ton of money and new management, a lot of people will soon be looking for new work.
B: I feel sorry for their _____. It'll be tough to find a new job.

B. Fill in the blanks in the sentences below with the words in the box. You may have to change the word form in the sentence.

persist	accountable	foresight	reputation
respect	adhere	maestro	exemplary

A: Welcome to HamaYama Fisheries today. First, let me give you some background about our firm. We were founded in 1979 by Densuke Hamazaki and Juzo Yamasaki.
B: Are they still active?
A: Presently, Mr. Yamasaki is our chairmen, but unfortunately Mr. Hamazaki died of a heart attack in 2001 and he is still missed. Mr. Hamazaki was an _____ leader, well known for his _____ and creative approach to the different setbacks we faced.
C: I heard that Mr. Yamasaki called him your _____.
A: Yes, that's right. Now let me return to our company and our philosophy. The _____ of our company's philosophy is providing excellent fish and seafood to all of our customers. This was the goal of Mr. Hamazaki and Mr. Yamasaki We are _____ to our customers, which we take very seriously.
C: Is that why you have the best _____. in the industry?
A: Yes, while we may not be the market leader in some categories we are the most respected. We _____ in always offering the best quality seafood and HamaYama will not lower our quality to offer cheaper products.
B: Has that strategy been successful?
A: I must first say that we take pride in _____ to our founders' values. Still keeping high standards has made it difficult at times but luckily we've acquired many foreign customers who care more for quality than price.

Writing Activity

Write an essay between 200-250 words on some topic that you have discussed in class. In your essay, try to use as many of the words below.

delicate	scope	corruption	allocations	reign
malaise	prominence	revered	catastrophic	out of left field
flaw	disruption	mentality	uniformity	label
inept	ardent	legacy	ostracize	entrench
convoluted	Byzantine	hinder	petty	subject
dynamic	produce	empire	obstacle	integration
anxious	immense	comprehensive	prone	abundance

Management Articles Vocabulary Review

Wonder Word Activity

Step One
Answer all the clues for the words in the columns below. Many of the words are from the vocabulary activities in the previous units. The words are also in the box of letters below.

1) Norway capital _ S _ _
2) Nickname for Richard _ _ _ k _
3) "Chicken _ r _ _ _ t"
4) "Beauty is in the _ _ _ of the beholder."
5) "The _ h _ _ e of things"
6) Toyota Prius e.g. . _ y _ d
7) What to do before a presentation _ r _ _
8) Huge i m _ _ _ _ _ _ e
9) Opposite of weak _ _ _ _ _ _
10) Rule _ e _ _ n
11) "Hold in high r _ g _ _"
12) Change _ _ d _ a _ _ _
13) Implement _ x _ _ _ t _
14) Stand up _ r _ _ e
15) Uncommon _ _ _ r _
16) 2 x quartet = o _ c _ _ _ t
17) "Poison _ _ _ l _ "
18) Land title _ _ e _ e _
19) Fault _ _ _ _ w
20) Incompetent _ _ n _ _ p _
21) Area _ _ _ o _ p _
22) Confusion _ c _ h _ _ _ _
23) Never stopping _ _ _ r _ i _ t _ n g
24) Peaceful s _ _ r _ _ _
25) Hurt _ a _ _ _
26) Quiz _ _ _ _
27) Look closely _ x _ _ _ _ n _
28) Embed _ n _ _ _ _ _ _ h
29) Craps needs _ _ i _ c _ _
30) Random _ c _ _ s memory
31) Inclined _ r _ _ _ e
32) Fantasy _ l _ _ _ _ _ _ n _
33) Be sorry _ e _ _ _ t
34) Police _ _ _ n _ up
35) Something for people to remember someone _ e _ _ a _ y _
36) Increase _ r _ _ _ _ h
37) Bring in illegally s _ _ g _ _ l _
38) Car damage _ _ _ n _
39) "_ _ _ Performance Indicator"

Step Two
All the words in the columns above appear in the box below. Scan the box below and search for a word. When you find a word, circle it. The words can be vertical, horizontal or diagonal. There will be seven letters remaining after you have found all the words. Unscramble those letters to spell the wonder word.

```
P R O N E A C C E S S I
R I S E X E C U T E S M
E C L B A B R E A S T M
P K O L M F L A W L R E
E Y E R I L L U S I O N
R C A I N E P T M R N S
S H A P E N E U U R G E
I A D A P T R E G A R D
S O I N C R R E G R E T
T S C O P E K D L E I E
I S E R E N E D E I G S
N L E G A C Y E D E N T
G R O W T H Y B R I D E
```

Wonder Word __ __ __ __ __ __ __

Management Articles Vocabulary Review

Presentation Activity
Make a presentation using at least eight of the words from the columns below. You may choose any topic for your presentation.

bombard	dilemma	advent	progress
vapid fluff	underlie	impede	relevant
sift	shaker	vapid fluff	fallacy
dashboard	boon	mountainous	trivial
grapple	disperse	transformative	empathy
buzzword	strain	glorify	usage
trumpet	diminish	commodity	private
civil liberties	empathy	prediction	conform

What Have You Learned So Far?
Write your thoughts on what the most interesting, most surprising, most controversial topic that you have discussed from the Management Articles Section.

Walk a Mile in My Shoes

Warm Up

Marketing Quotes
Do you agree with the quotes below? Give your answers and reasons below.

"Marketing is a contest for people's attention." -- Seth Godin
_____

"The aim of marketing is to know and understand the customer so well the product or service fits him and sells itself." -- Peter Drucker
_____

"Good marketing makes the company look smart. Great marketing makes the customer feel smart." – Joe Chernov
_____

"Unless your campaign has a big idea, it will pass like a ship in the night." -- David Ogilvy
_____

"Marketing is a core part of anything you do." –Keith Belling
_____

"Marketing takes a day to learn. Unfortunately, it takes a lifetime to master." --Phillip Kolter
_____

Vocabulary Finding Activity
A. Complete the phrases from the article
1. inadequate _____
2. carry out _____
3. vanguard _____
4. material _____
5. imperfection _____
6. insubstantial _____
7. flock _____
8. endless _____
9. predicament _____
10. configuration _____

B. Now, choose five of the words that you **found** from the above vocabulary activity and write five sentences below using the words in each sentence.
a) _____
b) _____
c) _____
d) _____
e) _____

Summarize the Article
Read the article and then summarize it in three sentences or less.
_____
_____
_____
_____
_____

Marketing Match
Match the 4Ps with their 4Cs counterparts

1. Product
2. Place
3. Promotion
4. Price

a) Communication
b) Customer
c) Cost
d) Channel

Walk a Mile in My Shoes

In most introductory marketing courses, students first learn the 4Ps of marketing (Also referred to as the marketing mix) price, product, place and promotion. Students are taught that for a marketing strategy to succeed, all these components must be factored in. Good marketers ask a multitude of questions: What is the product and will it do what customers expect? How much should the company charge for the product or service? How should the product be made available? How should the product be advertised?

In the early 80s some marketers realized that the 4P marketing mix was insufficient so they added three more Ps, people, process and physical evidence. Many marketing experts have highlighted people as a key component. As companies rely on people, they must have the right people to execute the marketing plan. For example if the sales force cannot close a sale then no matter how good the marketing mix was, it would still fail. People in the front lines need to be skilled or knowledgeable to implement the strategy.

The process element is concerned with the delivery of a service. Customers are usually present when receiving a good or service so how the product is delivered is part of what the consumer is paying for. Theme parks are a good example of how a consumer can experiences the process element. From the moment of buying a ticket, to entering through the gate, to interacting with staff, going on a ride, and using the washrooms, everything is part of the process.

Finally, the last P, physical evidence, is about what tangible item the customer gets to keep. That is easy for goods, but for services which are often intangible, customers may be looking at the surroundings or expect something concrete such as a brochure, memento or pamphlet.

While 4Ps and 7Ps make it easy for companies to organize their marketing strategy, they are flawed. The 4Ps marketing mix originated in the 1960s when homogeneous mass marketing was effective. Now markets are more segmented and consumers are savvier. Many consumers do not want to see themselves as part of the herd but as distinct individuals.

The second flaw is that the model focuses on the company and not on the customer. Take for example, the simple concept of price. In the 4P or 7P mix, companies often look at the prices they set in comparison to what its competitors are offering instead of looking at what the product costs the consumers. In these models, the company ignores the eternal customer dilemma of deciding how he or she is going to spend limited money to satisfy unlimited wants.

Because of these flaws, a new line of thinking emerged. Instead of using the 4P method, marketers should try to imagine themselves as consumers. Moreover, companies and their marketing staff should concentrate on not maximizing their gains, but on maximizing the customer's satisfaction and value. Therefore, they should ask how they could provide more value for the same cost to the customer instead of asking to make more profit from a product.

The newer marketing models, called the 4Cs, deem 'consumer-centricity' as the new strategy to marketing success. The primary focus is that a good or service is a solution for customers' needs. To understand what their needs and wants are marketers need to walk in their customers' shoes. By doing so, business people will become enlightened on what products consumers want to purchase.

If companies and their marketers start to integrate this concept into their marketing, they may avoid a common business blunder, marketing myopia. Marketing myopia starts when a firm's management first defines themselves by the products or services they offer. This myopia can lead to complacency and a loss of understanding what customers want or opportunities available.

Marketing myopia has felled many firms such as Kodak, Blackberry and Sharp. In the instance of Kodak, whose R&D department invented the digital camera, the company saw themselves as camera and film manufacturers and not the creators of images. However, with the rise of PCs and cell phones with their increased memory capacity, film was no longer needed.

Kodak failed to realize how customers viewed their product and that the demand for a physical reminder was plummeting. Their shortsightedness and inability to see things from the customer's point of view resulted in an American corporate icon, Kodak, no longer being in the industry that made it famous.

© David Baird

Walk a Mile in My Shoe

Activity Sheet

Reading Comprehension Activity

According to the reading, circle whether the statements below are true or false

1. Price, product, place and premonition make up the 4P marketing mix. — True/**False**
2. Four more components were added to the 4P marketing mix in the eighties. — True/**False**
3. Many consumers want to be seen as distinctive. — **True**/False
4. The 4P marketing mix takes into account that consumers have a limited amount of money to spend. — True/**False**
5. A company should concentrate on maximizing its customers' satisfaction and value, not on profit. — **True**/False
6. Marketing myopia is when a firm's management needs to wear glasses. — True/**False**
7. Kodak researchers developed the first digital camera. — **True**/False
8. Kodak, Blackberry and Sharp all suffered from long-sightedness. — True/**False**
9. Kodak was able to successfully adapt to the changes in the camera industry. — True/**False**

Vocabulary Activity

A. Match the words from the reading on the left with similar meaning words on the right

1. components
2. factored
3. savvier
4. interacting
5. homogeneous
6. concrete
7. deem
8. ignores
9. complacency
10. integrate
11. plummeting
12. icon

a) disregards
b) self-satisfaction
c) elements
d) taken into account
e) connecting
f) assimilate
g) plunging
h) symbol
i) uniform
j) solid
k) believe
l) sharper

B. Now, choose six of the words from the column on the left and write six sentences below using each of those words in a sentence.

Example: "Sho ga nai" is often used as an excuse for **complacency** in Japan.

a) _____
b) _____
c) _____
d) _____
e) _____
f) _____

Classroom Discussion Questions

1. Which companies do you think are consumer centric?
2. Which companies do you think are product centric?
3. What are the advantages and disadvantages of being consumer centric?
4. What are the advantages and disadvantages of being product centric?
5. What companies do you think suffer from marketing myopia?
6. Does your company have an accurate picture of how your customers view it?

Write discussion questions for class discussions based on the topic in the article.

1. _____
2. _____
3. _____

Walk a Mile in My Shoes Lesson Notes

_____
_____
_____
_____
_____
_____
_____
_____
_____
_____
_____
_____

Today's Vocabulary

Words	Synonym	Antonym	Definition

Collocations/Phrases	Definition

What did I learn today?
_____
_____
_____

What do I need to improve?
_____
_____
_____

My homework for next class
_____
_____
_____

© David Baird

Weapons of Mass Persuasion

Warm Up

Reading Comprehension
Scan the article to find the answers to the following questions.
1. What traditional media are mentioned in the article?
2. Who are Cicero, Cato and Aristotle?
3. What type of scientists study persuasion now?
4. Name three social media sites that are mentioned in the article.
5. Identify the four social media logos in the website.

Classroom Discussion Questions
1. Does marketing influence your purchasing decisions? If yes, how? If no, why not?
2. What is the best medium for advertising?
3. What is the worst medium for advertising?

Vocabulary Finding Activity
A. Complete the phrases from the article

a) word of _____
b) mass _____
c) integrated _____
d) control all _____
e) go _____ online
f) trial and _____
g) strenuous _____
h) channels of _____

B. Now, choose four of the phrases from the above vocabulary and then write four sentences below using the phrases in each sentence.
1. _____
2. _____
3. _____
4. _____

Vocabulary Matching Activity
A. Match the words from the article on the left with words and phrases of similar meaning on the right.

1. countless
2. bombarded
3. academics
4. trial and error
5. incorporating
6. facets
7. feedback
8. drawback
9. viral
10. drawbacks
11. strenuous

a) aspects
b) trending
c) numerous
d) overwhelmed
e) arduous
f) scholars
g) shortcoming
h) downside
i) reaction
j) hit and miss
k) integrating

B. Now, choose six of the words from the column on the left and write six sentences below using each of those words in a sentence. You may change the form of the words.
Example: *There are **countless** ways to improve my English.*

a) _____
b) _____
c) _____
d) _____
e) _____
f) _____

Weapons of Mass Persuasion

Today there are countless ways for people and organizations to deliver their message to their audience. There are flyers and tissues handed out in front of train stations, word of mouth, the Internet and social media, as well as traditional media, such as TV, radio, and newspapers. As there are so many methods, the result is people being bombarded by 600 messages a day. With so many messages to buy this and do that, it is becoming difficult for messages to be heard.

That is why studying persuasion is becoming increasingly important. At first, the study of persuasion was only done by academics who wanted to help improve people's writing or were studying Latin or Greek writers such as Cicero, Cato or Aristotle. Then in the late nineteenth century, mass production started which required mass advertising to generate demand from the public for their numerous products.

However, advertising is difficult to quantify. As Lord Leverhulme, the British industrialist said, "I know half my advertising isn't working, I just don't know which half." In the beginning, there was often no science involved in advertising, just trial and error. If it worked once, they would keep on doing it until it no longer worked. Marketers, copywriters and ad agencies then started to study persuasion to make their advertisements more effective

In the last few decades, science started to become more and more interested in persuasion, as business schools, psychologists, economists, political scientists and communication theorists started researching persuasion. The research has allowed people to understand, analyze and interpret the different facets of persuasion in greater depth. Presently in academics, a more integrated approach is utilized to study persuasion, incorporating many disciplines simultaneously.

The result of all this research is the creation of a multitude of theories and marketing has become more sophisticated and comprehensive. Marketers try to look at all facets of the persuasion process to make each step of their selling more effective.

Marketers' goals are to make the messenger look credible and sincere, have the message sound logical, the product look attractive and the company still control all facets of the message process. The latest medium to assist in performing these strenuous tasks and to attract potential customers is the Internet and more specifically, social media websites such as Facebook, Twitter and Tumblr.

Many Internet gurus and marketing consultants promote the idea that companies should create channels of communication by establishing a presence on social media platforms so their customers can give them feedback on their products. However, there is a drawback to this concept, as these sites now promote interaction with consumers, the feedback is not always positive.

The negative feedback can go viral which can damage a product's brand equity. It seems that every new communication channel also has its drawbacks

It seems that advertising in social media raises new questions. Is social media the new magic that will be able to sell products with incredible ease? Is the Internet changing how people react to products? Are the Internet ads being noticed? The truth is no matter what some Silicon Valley experts claim and predict, only time will tell what the Internet can truly do.

© David Baird

Weapons of Mass Persuasion Activity Sheet

Reading Comprehension Activity
According to the reading, circle whether the statements below are true or false

1. Communication can be sent to the public via the Internet and social media and mass media such as TV, radio and newspapers. — True/False
2. People are being flooded by 6,000 messages a day. — True/False
3. For centuries, only academics studied the concepts of persuasion. — True/False
4. Lord Leverhulme stated he never knew which part of his advertising was effective. — True/False
5. Many scholars are now researching persuasion from only their fields' perspective. — True/False
6. Marketing theories have become simpler and rougher. — True/False
7. Negative feedback can go viral online, which can mar a product's brand value. — True/False
8. Marketers now study all perspectives of the persuasion process. — True/False
9. Social media will let companies successfully sell their products effortlessly. — True/False

Social Media Marketing Plan Activity

You are working in the marketing department of a company that wants to use the Internet and social media to increase its brand awareness and help it introduce new products and services. With a partner, create a marketing strategy for your company. Afterwards present your ideas to the class.

Try to answer the following questions below when creating your website.
- What is your company and what does it sell?
- Who is your target audience?
- What is your end goal?
- Which social media platform do you want to use?
- How will the social media be integrated into your marketing strategy?
- How will you use social media?
- How will the social media be helpful to your strategy?
- How will the sites be maintained?
- What are the future possibilities?

Classroom Discussion Questions
Discuss the questions below with your classmates. Give your reasons.

1. Was Lord Leverhulme correct to say that it is too difficult to measure what part of marketing is effective? Give reasons
2. Do you think academics will ever clearly understand why people choose something?
3. How much does emotion influence your decisions?
4. Can marketers actually control all facets of the message process? Why do you think so?
5. How often do you use social member sites?
6. Have you ever bought anything from a social media website?
7. Is the Internet an effective medium for advertising?

Additional Questions for Discussion
Write discussion questions for class discussions based on the topic in the article.

a) _____
b) _____
c) _____
d) _____
e) _____

Weapons of Mass Persuasion Lesson Notes

_____
_____
_____
_____
_____
_____
_____
_____
_____
_____
_____

Today's Vocabulary

Words	Synonym	Antonym	Definition

Collocations/Phrases	Definition

What did I learn today?
_____
_____
_____
_____

What do I need to improve?
_____
_____
_____
_____

My homework for next class
_____
_____
_____

Parisian Love

Warm Up

YouTube Assignment
Before reading the article, watch the Parisian Love article on YouTube.
https://www.youtube.com/watch?v=nnsSUqgkDwU

Also, watch the Pakistan/India Google Ad.
https://www.youtube.com/watch?v=gHGDN9-oFJE

Marketing Quotes
Choose one of the marketing quotes below and explain to your partner why you agree or disagree with it.
- "If you build a better mousetrap, the world will beat a path to your door."
- "A man who stops advertising to save money is like a man who stops a clock to save time."
- "If you don't like what's being said, change the conversation."
- "Don't find customers for your products, find products for your customers."
- "I know half my advertising isn't working, I just don't know which half."

Create an Ad
Choose any product and with some classmates create a TV advertisement. Use the boxes below to help you plan the TV spot.

Sound:	Sound:	Sound:
Script:	Script:	Script:
Sound:	Sound:	Sound:
Script:	Script:	Script:

Parisian Love

During the 2010 Super Bowl broadcast, Google ran its first advertisement for its market leading search engine. The clever TV spot called Parisian Love reached over 106 million people that day. The straightforward ad showcased how easy and efficient the company's search engine is to use, while simultaneously telling a love story. It reminded the 106 million-sized audience that Google's vaunted search engine is an indispensable enabler of modern life.

The ad was special for many reasons, as Google had rarely used TV to advertise as they thought the Internet was sufficient and they saw no need to interact with other media. Second, they believed that if you build a better mousetrap, the world will beat a path to your door. Google's CEO Eric Schmidt had said on many occasions that its company's dominant market share was earned by quality of searches, not by advertising. Still Google was becoming a little worried as Yahoo and Bing were cutting into Google's market share with aggressive advertising campaigns.

In addition, the commercial was not what you expected from Google. Google is a company that believes in logic, numbers and algorithms, not one associated with sentiment. Google used a romantic story to sell its search engine; not numbers to tell people how superior and accurate their search engine is compared to their competitors.

Why did Google tell a story? Because stories stick in people's minds and they create an emotional response and connection. Stories can be magical as they take people to a place where they want to go. A story has a beginning, middle and end, which make them easy to follow and remember.

Human beings' brains are wired to remember stories according to neurologists and psychologists probably because the human race has been telling and listening to stories for thousands of years. Stories started when cavemen were sitting around the fire at night telling tales of the various hunts. After the hunting tales ended, they moved on to create myths to explain the stars, moon and nature. At the same time, primitive man began using stories to include messages and warnings.

Stories continued being used for telling messages as great religious leaders like Buddha, Jesus Christ and Confucius employed this technique in their parables. In our modern age, countless business presentation experts also strongly advocate the importance of using a story when presenting.

Advertisers realized the importance of the story and began using stories first in illustrations then radio and later TV. They now recognize the importance of the stores ability to resonate with an audience and stick in the consumers' mind. In marketing, stickiness, having something stick in the consumer's mind about your product is valuable. Having the consumer remember your product tied to a positive emotion is priceless.

Looking at the Google commercial, we can see why it was successful. It connected to the audience by using something people are familiar with love, relationships and marriage yet told the story in a unique and entertaining way. Moreover, it was easy to follow so the audience was not confused.

Even today, years after the ad first ran the message is still strong as it effectively highlighted the elegance and simplicity of Google's search capabilities. Even more important for Google, Google is still the number one search engine.

© David Baird

Parisian Love

Activity Sheet

Reading Comprehension Activity

According to the reading, circle whether the statements below are true or false

1. In 2010, Google ran its first ever advertisement. — True/False
2. Google's CEO often said that it lead the market because its search engine was very good. — True/False
3. Yahoo and Bing increased their market share in 2009 and 2010. — True/False
4. Google used numbers and logic to sell its search engine in its ads. — True/False
5. Many famous religious leaders have used stories to tell a message. — True/False
6. Human beings' brains are designed and organized to remember stories. — True/False
7. Ad agencies only used stories when TV became established. — True/False
8. Google is still the number one search engine. — True/False

Vocabulary Matching Activity

A. Match the words from the reading on the left with similar meaning words on the right

1. showcased
2. simultaneously
3. indispensable
4. vaunted
5. sufficient
6. algorithms
7. wired
8. resonate
9. advocate
10. parables

a) at the same time
b) exulted
c) echo
d) complex math equations
e) encourage
f) highlighted
g) fables
h) designed
i) plenty
j) essential

B. Now, choose five of the words from the above vocabulary exercise on the left and write five sentences below using each of those words in a sentence. You may change the form of the words.
Example: *Speaking English has become **indispensable** in business.*

a) _____
b) _____
c) _____
d) _____
e) _____

Classroom Discussion Questions

Please discuss the questions below with your classmates. Ask your classmates follow up questions if needed. Moreover, give detailed reasons to your answers.

1. Do you use Google's search engine? Why or why not?
2. Are search engines an indispensable enabler of modern life?
3. Are stories as powerful as the writer says they are?
4. Do you think there is a difference between the qualities of the various search engines?
5. What parable has influenced you the most?
6. What commercial has stuck in your mind?
7. What do you think is the most powerful emotion to use in a commercial?
8. What is priceless for a business?

Write discussion questions for class discussions based on the topic in the article.

1. _____
2. _____
3. _____
4. _____
5. _____
6. _____

Parisian Love Lesson Notes

_____
_____
_____
_____
_____
_____
_____
_____
_____
_____

Today's Vocabulary

Words	Synonym	Antonym	Definition

Collocations/Phrases	Definition

What did I learn today?
_____
_____
_____
_____

What do I need to improve?
_____
_____
_____
_____

My homework for next class
_____
_____
_____

© David Baird

The Eternal Marketing Buzzword Brand

Warm Up

Brands and Slogans
Match the brand names on the left with their slogan on the right
1. Nike
2. Subway
3. Apple
4. BMW
5. Panasonic
6. Nestle
7. Toyota
8. Nintendo

a) Ideas for life
b) Think differently
c) Let's go places
d) Good Food. Good Life
e) Who are you?
f) The ultimate driving machine
g) Just do it
h) Eat fresh

Classroom Discussion Questions
1. Name three popular brands from different industries.
2. Describe your image of the three brands.
3. Why are brand names important?
4. Do you think brands are important? Why or why not?

Vocabulary Match Activity
A. Match the expressions from the article on the left with the definitions on the right.
1. brand loyalty
2. brand awareness
3. brand image
4. brand communities
5. personal branding
6. co-branding

a) The extent to which consumers are familiar with the qualities of a particular brand
b) Two companies work together to create marketing synergy.
c) A group of people formed on the basis of attachment to a product.
d) Consumers being steadfast to a brand and making repeated purchases.
e) The impression in the consumers' mind of a brand's real and imaginary personality.
f) The practice of people marketing themselves and their careers as brands.

B. Put the expressions in the left column into the sentences below.
1. Uniqlo is a unique clothing retailer as it does not use its clothes to raise _____.
2. Some critics say _____ is people just making clever remarks to differentiate themselves.
3. The Nike app on the Apple iPod is a great example of _____.
4. _____ changes upon which part of the population you ask.
5. Apple has a very large _____ with its Mac user groups being one example.
6. Tobacco companies enjoy the highest _____ in marketing.

Description Activity
What adjectives and attributes would you use to describe the following brands?

Toyota _____   Coca-Cola _____
Disney _____   McDonalds _____
Amazon _____   Uniqlo _____
IKEA _____   ANA _____
Softbank _____   Canon _____
Sony _____   MOS Burger _____

What do these buzzwords mean?
Define the following business expressions below.
synergy _____   buy –in _____
scalable _____   empower _____
ecosystem _____   escalate _____
think outside the box _____
corporate values _____

The Eternal Marketing Buzzword: Brand

Every few years marketing has a new buzzword such as storytelling, showrooming, touch point, and eating your own dog food, which they often overuse. Still one word is not new but is still sexy: brand. If a marketer wants to impress the boss or client, he or she can just inject brand or branding into the discussion and presto, dazzled clients.

Now there are some expressions that even a first-year commerce student can understand such as "brand awareness" or "brand loyalty," but other expressions can cause even the most experienced business people to Google a definition for. Advertisers will talk about a brand voice or persona and the need for branding strategy and brand communities.

There are many more examples of marketers' overuse of the word, but the question is, "Why do they love the word brand?" Wikipedia defines brand as the "name, term, design, symbol, or any other feature that identifies one seller's product distinct from those of another seller." Simple, but why is this word overused so much?

The first reason is a brand is more than its name, logo, slogan, shape and color. A brand's greatest value is its image. Creating a successful brand image means positioning the brand where consumers have a positive emotional response to it. The brand needs to be attractive to consumers on an emotional level so they will take pleasure in buying that product every time. When the brand reaches that level, it is a very valuable intangible asset, which makes it very sexy.

Take for instance, Coca-Cola, the world's most successful brand. What do people think of when they see a Coca-Cola logo or bottle? Is it a high calorie, sweet, carbonated soft drink or the product that promises fun, freedom and refreshment, with a nostalgic connection? Probably the latter, so that is why Coca-Cola is number one.

Along with sending an emotional message easily and quickly to consumers, a popular brand possesses two other traits: consistency and trust. When someone buys a brand product, they expect a certain amount of consistency and quality with each purchase. If the consistency is maintained, the customer returns, as they trust the brand. The result for the company is brand loyalty.

As powerful a tool and important a brand is, it is also not often under the company's control. A brand is how people feel about a product or company. No matter how a company markets itself, no matter how hard it tries, it simply cannot control what someone else feels. In addition, people's perception of a product can change. For instance, Corvette once was seen as an iconically cool car, but later became a symbol of a man's mid-life crisis. GM could not control how people felt about its car.

Furthermore, if the company screws up through scandal or major product defect, consumers can lose trust in the brand. The company's business strategy must also match its brand strategy. You cannot say one thing and then do something else.

GAP is an example of a company whose business strategy did not match its brand strategy. GAP was a very popular retailer, as it offered stylish fashion basics for baby boomers and teenagers. Then its designs became drab and dreary and it did not rotate its inventory as often. As a result, its customer base no longer considers GAP trendy, so its sales have been sliding.

Marketers, brand managers and all members of an organization's leadership have to do two simple things, first combine focus, discipline and execution to create a positive brand image; second be consistent so you do not undermine your first stratagy. Do those two things and the business will have a strong brand that lasts for years.

© David Baird

The Eternal Marketing Buzzword, Brand

Activity Sheet

True or False

Based on the reading, circle whether the answers are true or false.
1. Storytelling, showrooming and touch point are popular marketing jargon. — True/False
2. Brands are living beings as they have a voice, persona and identity. — True/False
3. Talking about brand will impress your bosses. — True/False
4. The meaning of brand is a product that has a name, term, design and symbol. — True/False
5. Popular brands have credibility. — True/False
6. Coca Cola's image promises fun, freedom, and being American. — True/False
7. The Gap has successfully maintained its brand over the last ten years. — True/False
8. Business strategy and brand strategy can work separately. — True/False

Vocabulary Match Activity

A. Match the words from the article on the left with the synonyms on the right.

1. buzzword   a) view
2. persona   b) dull
3. presto   c) cliché
4. intangible   d) fault
5. nostalgic   e) damage
6. perception   f) sentimental
7. defect   g) change
8. drab   h) character
9. rotate   i) indefinable
10. undermine   j) magically

B. Now, choose five of the words from the left column and write five sentences below using each of those words in a sentence.
Example: Benchmarking has become a popular business *buzzword*.

a) _____
b) _____
c) _____
d) _____
e) _____

Classroom Discussion Questions

Please discuss the questions below with your classmates. Ask your classmates follow-up questions if needed. In addition, give detailed reasons to your answers.

1. What recent buzzword or expression do you like?
2. What recent buzzword or expression do you dislike?
3. How would you define brand?
4. What product do you think has a strong brand?
5. What product do you think has a poor brand image?
6. Which is more important brand strategy or business strategy?
7. Do you know any examples where brand strategy and business strategy clashed?

Write additional questions for discussion based on the topic in the article.

1. _____
2. _____
3. _____
4. _____
5. _____

The Eternal Marketing Buzzword, Brand
Lesson Notes

Today's Vocabulary

Words	Synonym	Antonym	Definition

Collocations/Phrases	Definition

What did I learn today?

What do I need to improve?

My homework for next class

Marketing Articles Vocabulary Review

Fill in the blanks in the conversation with the words in the box.

rational	entitled	prevail	harmony	sufficient
advocating	indispensable	unverified	premises	

A: People are _____ to their own opinions.
B: But if your opinion is based on _____ facts and false _____ then the opinion is not reasonable.
A: That's a matter of opinion.
B: No, we are supposed to be _____ people where judgment and decisions are based on reason, not feeling.
A: If it seems to be true or feels true, then it's probably true.
B: So you are _____ that we should ignore logic and common sense?
A: No, I am trying to say is that people make decisions and come up with opinions and ideas based on emotions so the emotions must be respected.
B: Does respected mean that emotions should _____ over logic?
A: No, but when a decision is made, the feelings of all stakeholders should be taken into account. _____ and consensus should be the goal.
B But will that always get _____ results?
A: Not quickly, so patience will be _____.

buzzwords	countless	bombarded	branding
gurus	resonate	rephrase	jargon

B: I am feeling so confused these days.
A: Why? What's up?
B: I've been listening to some marketing executives give _____ presentations and I just don't understand their _____ they have _____ us with.
B: For example?
A: They talk about the need to concentrate on downstream and not be so upstream. It sounds like they are talking about fishing not marketing.
A: Marketing people enjoy incorporating the latest _____ to make themselves sound knowledgeable and important. It's part of their personal _____.
B: That's a cynical thing to say.
A: Let me _____ that. Some marketing gurus know what they are talking about, while others just parrot what the _____ are saying.
A: So how can you tell the difference between the real ones and the fakes?
B: Simple, just ask them tough questions about their presentation. The one whose answers _____ with you, are probably the real deal.

perception	facets	approach	techniques
feedback	argued	drawbacks	

A: Before the training, what was your _____ going in?
B: I thought it would be more academic where we would just sit and listen.
A: And now what's your view?
B: Well the trainer used many inventive _____ that I didn't expect. While she did lecture on the different _____ of quality customer service, and we had some lively debates, instructive role-plays about customer service. At the end we had a great _____ session.
A: Debates?
B: Yeah, we _____ over whether the customer is always right.
A: Who won?
B: It was a draw.
A: Were there any _____ to the training?
B: One it was too short and two, my whole team should have attended it. It will be hard for me to get my team on board with this new _____ without them having attended the training.
A: Understood.

Marketing Articles Vocabulary Review

Dialogue Writing Activity

With a classmate, write a dialogue with people talking about brands or marketing. Your dialogue must contain 12 of the words from the words below.

bombarded	academics	trial and error	incorporating
feedback	drawback	viral	drawbacks
assertion	strenuous	showcased	simultaneously
coined	indispensable	speculation	conventional
exulted	sufficient	algorithms	wired
sway	icon	beliefs	booming
resonate	facet	advocate	parables
loyalty	awareness	image	brand communities
personal branding	co-branding	buzzword	persona
presto	intangible	nostalgic	perception
defect	drab	rotate	undermine
unverified	entitled	perception	premise
euphoria	irrational	clouded	complacency
isolating	word of mouth	trial and error	

Dialogue

Marketing Articles Vocabulary Review

Sentence Rewriting Activity

Multiple short sentences in a paragraph are difficult for people to follow as they stop and start too much. Sentences should be combined so all sentences are not brief and of equal length.

Three common methods to combine sentences are coordination, subordination and reduction.
Coordination is a way of adding sentences together and we use words such as *and, or, but* and *so*.

Example: I bought a ticket. I went to the concert.
Combined: I bought a ticket and I went to the concert.

Subordination is combining sentences that makes one sentence more important than the other sentence, from an independent clause to a dependent clause by adding such words as *when, although, if* (called subordinating conjunctions) or such words as *when, what,* or *that* (called relative pronouns).

Example: We looked in the back of the cupboard. Janet will often hide Pringles containers in the back of the cupboard.
Combined: We looked in the back of the cupboard, where Janet will often hide Pringles containers.

Reduction is going further by reducing the subordinate clauses in the sentence into a phrase.

Example: Ms. Tanaka is a well-known financial advisor. She is an outstanding applicant for our executive loan officer at our bank.
Combined and Reduced: Ms. Tanaka, a well-known financial advisor, is an outstanding applicant for our executive loan officer at our bank.

Combine the following group of short sentences below to make longer sentences.

1. A brand needs to be attractive to consumers. It should be attractive on an emotional level.

2. GAP is a very popular retailer. It offers stylistic fashion basics. It sells to baby boomers and teenagers.

3. Google is a company. It believes in logic, numbers and algorithms. People do not associate Google with sentiment.

4. Marketers try to look at all facets of the persuasion process. Marketers try to make each step of their selling process more effective.

5. Kodak was shortsighted. It did not have the ability to see things from the customer's point of view. Their lack of skilled resulted in Kodak failing. Kodak has left the camera industry. It was a famous company in the camera industry. Kodak is an American corporate icon.

6. We called his position Regional Marketing Manager. In reality, he was a glorified errand boy. He was a paper pusher.

7. Marketers should indentify what obstacles are blocking customer satisfaction. Examples of obstacles could be competitors, barriers to entry, and budgets.

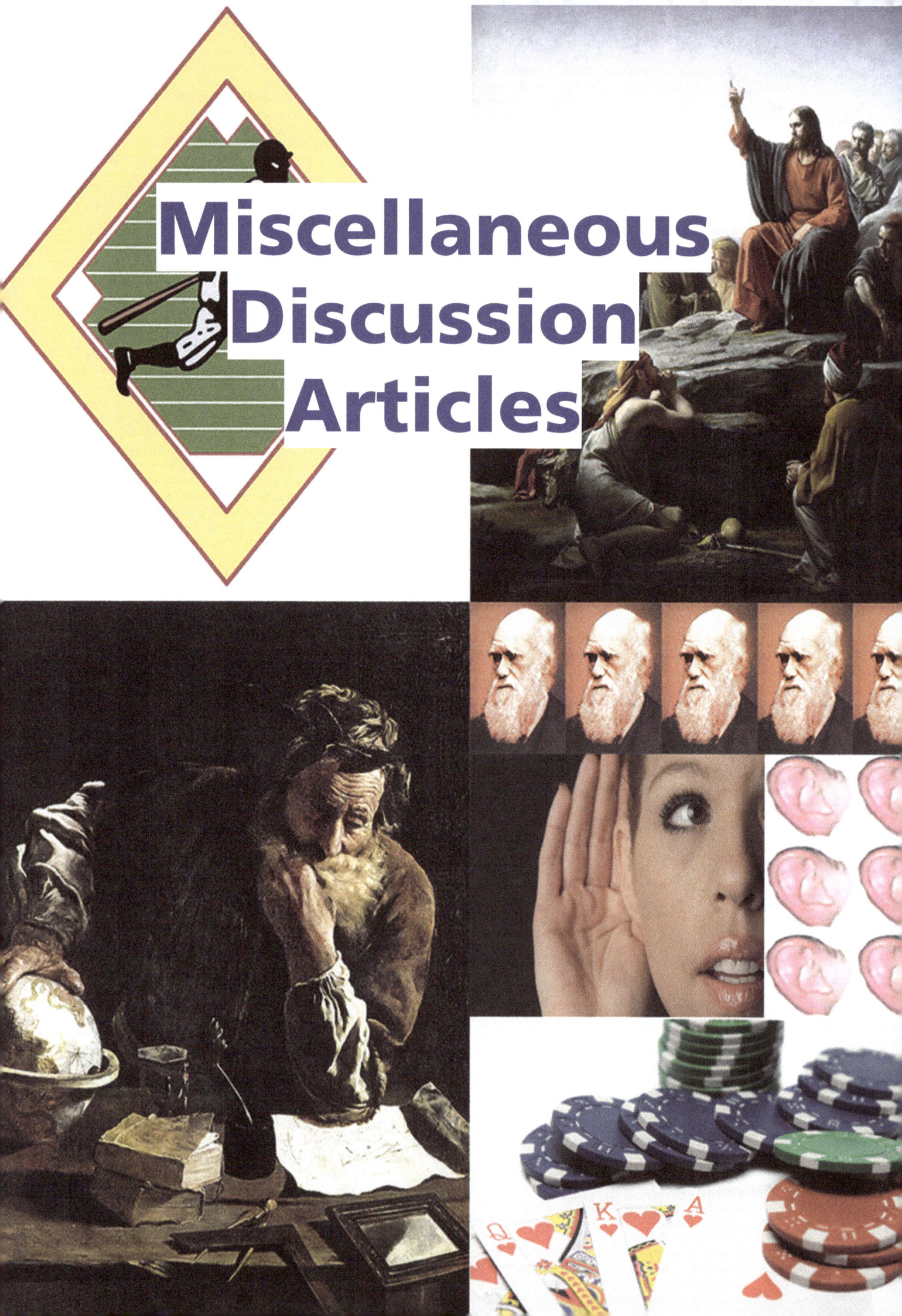

The Disease of Not Listening

Warm Up

Classroom Discussion Questions
1. What do you think makes a good listener?
2. Do you think you are a good listener? Why or why not?
3. On a scale of 1 to 10 (1 being the best and 10 being the worst) how would you rate your listening skills?
4. Who is the best listener you know? Why do you think they are so good?
5. Who listens to you?

Good Listening Tips
Fill in the blanks with the words in the box below.

clarify	ask	attentive	remember
listening	react	maintain	interrupt

_____ eye contact
Make _____ sounds
Do not _____ too much
_____ follow-up questions

Have _____ body language
_____ appropriately
_____ if needed
_____ what the speaker said

Listen vs. Hear Activity
Fill in the blanks with either *listen* or *hear*. Make sure to use the proper verb tense.
1. We should _____ to what he wants to say.
2. I don't really think you _____ me.
3. She often _____ voices so people think she is a little crazy.
4. Have you _____ about the changes to the procedures?
5. Just watch and _____ to what he does.
6. The children _____ with interest to his amazing stories.
7. I would be interested to _____ what you have to say.
8. I need to _____ to the radio.
9. His students often do not closely _____ to his lectures.
10. I was sorry to _____ about your divorce.

Listening Quotes Activity
With a partner, paraphrase the following quotes.

1. "Education is the ability to listen to almost anything without losing your temper or your self-confidence."
    Robert Frost
   _____
   _____

2. "We have two ears and one mouth so that we can listen twice as much as we speak."
    Epictetus
   _____
   _____

3. "Listen to what you know instead of what you fear."
    Richard Bach
   _____
   _____

4. "It is greed to do all the talking but not to want to listen at all."
    Democritus
   _____
   _____

The Disease of Not Listening

Effective communication is an acquired skill that goes two ways, speaking and listening so in a conversation the speaking time goal should be 50/50. However, the result is seldom achieved. Why? For the simple reason that most people want to talk about themselves and their opinions. Therefore, when people meet an attentive listener, they will be happy because they will get a chance to speak.

For example, have you ever had this type of conversation?
"I had a great conversation with Masahiro at the party."
"Really, Chie, what did you talk about?"
"We talked about my trip to Kyoto and discussed my favorite temples and shrines."
"Has Masahiro ever gone to Kyoto?"
"You know, I never asked."

Most people are often like Chie that if they meet a great listener they then think that the listener was a great conversationalist. In Dale Carnegie's very famous book "*How to Win Friends and Influence People,*" he gives many anecdotes highlighting the importance of being a good listener. He saw listening as an important social skill that was an easy way to build a bridge between people.

Our inability to listen is often at the cause of our relationship difficulties whether at work or in our personal life. Not attentively listening shows a lack of respect to the speaker that makes creating a successful relationship difficult. Even if you do respect them, the action of not being a good listener shows otherwise. For instance, if you look at your smart phone, fidget or do not make eye contact, you are giving the message that the other person does not count. These actions as Shakespeare once wrote are the disease of not listening, and the malady of marking (not paying attention).

Given its significance and helpfulness, why do people seldom listen to each other? Some simple reasons could be a person having a hearing problem or the speaker could not be speaking loud enough. These problems can be easily overcome by speaking up, speaking more clearly or the listener buying a hearing aid.

However, other barriers to good listening habits may be more difficult to overcome, such as ones of attitude or culture. Of those two, attitude is the biggest obstacle to surmount. Attitude is based on personality. To change listening habits, people have to make a conscious effort to change themselves, which is never an easy task.

The disease of not listening can be cured with an adjustment of attitude. First try to understand that good listening as Dale Carnegie stated, is a form of appreciation and everyone wishes to be appreciated. It does not matter if the person is a billionaire CEO of a major conglomerate or a minimum wage worker; they all want to be listened to. Being a capable listener can turn customers into allies, angry spouses into happy ones, or enemies into friends. Once you have adjusted your attitude, you can start becoming a good listener

After adjusting your attitude, you must concentrate on what the other person is saying and forget your problems and worries. Focus on the speaker, not on yourself. Do not be quick to judge or anger nor try to impress the speaker with your knowledge. Allow them to finish and try not to jump to conclusions or fill in their pauses. Try not to see the discussion as a competition, but as a time to exchange ideas and to learn.

Skills that you will need for being a good listener are maintaining eye contact, not doing anything else and letting the other person finish. Interrupting should only be done to paraphrase, clarify and show that you are listening.

However, do not forget the most important rule for good listening: remember what the other person said. Now the question is; do you now want to make the effort to listen?

© David Baird

The Disease of Not Listening

Activity Sheet

True or False Quiz

Based on the reading, circle whether the statements below are true or false.

1. To be a good conversationalist you should try to speak more than the other person does. — True/False
2. *How to Win Friends and Influence People* was written by Andrew Carnegie. — True/False
3. Shakespeare called not paying attention, the malady of marking. — True/False
4. The biggest problem to overcome for good listening is a person's outlook. — True/False
5. Good listening is a form of admiration. — True/False
6. A good listener should jump to conclusions to help speed the conversation along. — True/False
7. Conversation is a competition where the person who speaks the most wins. — True/False
8. People should interrupt to change the subject or clarify. — True/False

Vocabulary Match

A. Match the words from the reading on the left with the words that have a similar meaning from the words on the right

1. acquired
2. goal
3. anecdotes
4. cure
5. surmount
6. obvious
7. obstacle
8. appreciation
9. adjusted
10. conglomerate

a) target
b) clear
c) overcome
d) heal
e) problem
f) attained
g) changed
h) stories
i) consortium
j) admiration

B. Choose five of the words from the above vocabulary exercise on the left side and write five sentences below using each of those words in a sentence.

a) _____
b) _____
c) _____
d) _____
e) _____

Classroom Discussion Questions

Please discuss the questions below with your classmates. Give detailed answers and ask follow-up questions when necessary.

1. Have you ever read Dale Carnegie's book, "*How to Win Friends and Influence People*"? If no, would you like to read it?
2. Do you feel appreciated or unappreciated?
3. What is the biggest obstacle to good listening? How can people overcome it?
4. Have you ever jumped to conclusions when listening? Was it helpful or harmful?
5. How would you teach good listening habits to someone?
6. Do you think there are differences between listening attitudes in different cultures?
7. What advice would you give to a non-native speaker of your language on how they should listen?

Write discussion questions for class discussion based on the topic in the article.

a) _____
b) _____
c) _____
d) _____
e) _____

The Disease of Not Listening
Lesson Notes

_____
_____
_____
_____
_____
_____
_____
_____
_____
_____

Today's Vocabulary

Words	Synonym	Antonym	Definition

Collocations/Phrases	Definition

What did I learn today?
_____
_____
_____
_____

What do I need to improve?
_____
_____
_____
_____

My homework for next class
_____
_____
_____

Play the Man Across From You

Warm Up

Poker Phrase Match

Match the phrase with the definition on the right

1. Upping the ante
2. Keeping his cards close to his vest
3. Overplaying their hand
4. Lay/put our cards on the table
5. Bluffing
6. An ace in the hole

a) Being guarded in dealing with people and a little secretive
b) An unforeseen or secret resource.
c) Make a frank and clear revelation such what you need or want.
d) Misleading someone by a show of strength or confidence.
e) Spoil one's chance of success through excessive confidence in one's position.
f) Raising the cost or risk of an activity.

Choose three of the expressions from the above vocabulary exercise and write three sentences below using each of the phrases in a sentence.

1. _____
2. _____
3. _____

Negotiation Skills Survey

Look at all the qualities below and rank them by importance to be a good negotiator. **1** is the highest and **25** is the least important. Then discuss your answers with your classmates.

Quality	Ranking
1. Be knowledgeable about what is negotiated	_____
2. Plan effectively and thoroughly	_____
3. Be open to alternatives	_____
4. Listen well.	_____
5. Know what you want.	_____
6. Know what you need	_____
7. Know what your counterpart needs	_____
8. Know what your counterpart wants	_____
9. Be able to compromise	_____
10. Go with the flow during the negotiation	_____
11. Be patient.	_____
12. Be persistent.	_____
13. Keep emotions in check.	_____
14. Have strong problem solving skills.	_____
15. Keep negotiations friendly.	_____
16. Try to read people's feelings	_____
17. Don't be easily intimidated	_____
18. Be willing to ask questions	_____
19. Push hard to make an agreement	_____
20. Look at the negotiation as a zero sum contest	_____
21. Build trust with your counterpart	_____
22. Try to get everything you want	_____
23. Do not give out any information	_____
24. Speak loudly and quickly	_____
25. Clarify authority quickly	_____

Play the Man Across From You

There are hundreds of books and experts that offer advice on negotiation, but there is one game that is often cited as an activity to learn negotiation skills. It is not chess, mahjong or backgammon, but poker. Poker is now seen as a game of skill, not as a game of chance.

Poker, while always a popular game, became even more fashionable with the rise of two new communication phenomena: cable TV and the Internet. As more and more channels popped up there has been a high demand for content. ESPN the 24-hour sports cable network started the new wave of popularity by televising the World Series of Poker and creating the hole-card camera, which helped turn poker into a spectator sport. As a result, the World Series of Poker Purse, which was at $1,000,000 in 1991, rose to about $9,000,000 by 2011.

People seeing the large money being wagered on TV and how effortless it looked to play, thought they could easily become world-class poker players. To make it easy for these big time poker wannabes to practice their skills, the Internet at that time brought poker into their homes. Internet poker sites started to pop up which allowed any player to pay 5 to 10 games at a time so you could quickly win or lose a fair amount of money every night. It was estimated that the online poker revenues grew from $82.7 million in 2001 to $2.4 billion in 2005. Unfortunately, for the many poker site owners and online players, many sites were forced to close in 2006 because of newly enacted US legislation.

Nevertheless, even before this all happened, poker expressions and sayings had become part of everyday English vocabulary and are often used in business. The ante which is the payment required to join a poker game is used in a few common idioms. For example *upping the ante* means raising the cost or risk of an activity. Another poker phrase, *keeping your cards close to your vest* means to be very guarded and a little secretive when dealing with people. At the end of each hand, we *lay/put our cards on the table*, which also means to make a frank and clear revelation such as what you need or want.

Bluffing another popular poker expression is one of the most common tactics in poker. To bluff is to mislead someone by a show of strength or confidence. You make the other players believe that your hand is better than it truly is. In poker, a pure bluff is usually betting a substantial amount on your weak hand making your opponents afraid, so they then fold. The result is you win the pot. Bluffing has intrigued economists and mathematicians who have used game theory to calculate what the optimal amount of bluffing is.

In business, bluffing should be a nuanced deception not a bold lie. One example of bluffing in business is making your counterpart believe that you offer the best services and you would have no regret about leaving the negotiation. Your confidence implies that you have other customers craving your services. While, in fact, there may be better services available in the market and you are in desperate need of work.

There is one more simple strategy that many poker players have which could be applied in negotiations. In Casino Royale, James Bond states one of the most important rules for poker and a very good one for negotiation, "You never play your hand. You play the man across from you." This sage advice tells you that it is more important to observe and react to your negotiation counterpart than it is to worry about what you have or need. Remember that advice the next time you are sitting across from you boss negotiating your salary.

© David Baird

Play the Man Across From You

Activity Sheet

True or False Quiz

Based on the reading, circle whether the answers are true or false.
1. Chess is seen as the best game for honing your negotiation skills. — True/False
2. The World Series of Poker Purse was $90,000,000 by 2011. — True/False
3. Soon after the beginning of the century, online poker became quite popular. — True/False
4. Many poker websites shut down in 2006 because of new American laws. — True/False
5. *Ante* means you are against poker. — True/False
6. *Putting your cards on the table* means to truthfully state what you know or want. — True/False
7. Ecologists and mathematicians have become fascinated by bluffing. — True/False
8. Game theory is used to determine optimal times to bluff. — True/False
9. The article advises business people to aggressively bluff. — True/False
10. James Bond was given good advice for playing poker in Casino Royale. — True/False

Vocabulary Match Activity

A. Match the words from the article on the left with the synonyms on the right.

1. cited
2. wagered
3. wannabes
4. world-class
5. guarded
6. revelation
7. tactics
8. optimal
9. intrigued
10. nuanced
11. craving
12. sage

a) cautious
b) disclosure
c) gambits
d) named
e) fascinated
f) desire
g) hopefuls
h) wise
i) outstanding
j) refined
k) bet
l) most advantageous

B. Choose six of the words from the above vocabulary exercise and write six sentences below using each of those words in a sentence.

Example: The servers here are mainly *wannabe* actors.

a) _____
b) _____
c) _____
d) _____
e) _____
f) _____

Classroom Discussion Questions

Please discuss the questions below with your classmates. Ask follow up questions if needed and give detailed answers.
1. What makes a successful gambler? Are you a good at gambling?
2. Have you ever played poker? If yes, did you win or lose?
3. Do you think poker can help teach people become successful negotiators?
4. Do you have a good poker face?
5. Have you ever overplayed your hand?
6. Is keeping your cards always close to your vest a good business practice?
7. Is bluffing a good tactic in business?
8. How would you evaluate your negotiation skills? What are your strengths and weaknesses?
9. How is a successful negotiator similar to a successful gambler? How are they different?
10. Do you agree with the advice, "You never play your hand, you play the man across from you?"

Write discussion questions for class discussions based on the topic in the article.

a) _____
b) _____
c) _____
d) _____
e) _____

Play the Man Across From You

Lesson Notes

_____
_____
_____
_____
_____
_____
_____
_____
_____
_____

Today's Vocabulary

Words	Synonym	Antonym	Definition

Collocations/Phrases	Definition

What did I learn today?
_____
_____
_____
_____

What do I need to improve?
_____
_____
_____
_____

My homework for next class
_____
_____
_____

The Golden Rule

Warm Up

Complete the Proverb

A. Match the beginning of the well-known proverbs on the left with the ending on the right column. Write your answers in the line below.

1. The pen is mightier _____
2. Don't bite the hand _____
3. The squeaky wheel _____
4. If at first you don't succeed _____
5. People who live in glass houses _____
6. Beggars can't _____
7. When the blind lead the blind, _____
8. You can't teach an old dog _____
9. Love of money _____
10. The spirit is willing, _____

a) should not throw stones.
b) but the flesh is weak.
c) new tricks.
d) than the sword.
e) be choosers.
f) Is the root of all evil.
g) they fall both into a ditch.
h) gets the grease.
i) try, try again.
j) that feeds you.

B. Now choose three of the sayings from the above exercise and write an explanation of what these sayings mean.

1. _____

2. _____

3. _____

Vocabulary Finding Activity

A. Find words in the article that mean the following

1. proverb _____
2. boring _____
3. incompetence _____
4. build _____
5. surpass _____
6. considerably _____
7. boost _____
8. togetherness _____
9. unprofessional _____
10. significant _____
11. assessment _____
12. connected _____

B. Now, choose six of the words from your answers in the above vocabulary exercise and write six sentences below using each of those words in a sentence.

a) _____
b) _____
c) _____
d) _____
e) _____
f) _____

C. Look at the article and come up with definition and an example of four of the following terms. If needed, use a dictionary.

a) fall on deaf ears   b) a jumping off point   c) strong emotional bond
d) stage fright   e) a waste of time   f) glazed over

a) _____

b) _____

c) _____

d) _____

The Golden Rule

In the Bible, Jesus preached to his followers "Do unto others as you would have them to do unto you." This moral maxim is known as the Golden Rule, which is a central message of Jesus' teaching. This is not just a Christian precept, but it can be found in all major religions. It means treat other people as you would like to be treated. It also means not to treat people in ways you would not want to be treated.

The Golden Rule should also be applied to presentations. If you do not want to listen to a lackluster presentation then do not give one. By you giving one less dull speech, there will be one less audience who will have to endure another tedious talk. The interesting speech will have made someone else's day more productive and more interesting.

Why is giving an appealing business presentation so important? In sales, a presentation's success depends upon your presentation outshining the competition. Your organization and your product are judged on how you deliver a presentation. A poor sales pitch to a potential client means no sales. Additionally your company will be viewed as amateurish and a waste of time to do business with.

Inside the company, presentations are important as poor presentations can cause your colleagues to leave a meeting feeling bored and frustrated and resulting in them dreading watching your next presentation. On the other hand, an engaging speech will forge a strong emotional bond between the presenter and the audience. A significant by-product generated from a first-rate speech will create a camaraderie that can stimulate and uplift co-workers.

Your presentations will first be judged by how well you communicate your message. Additionally, strong presentation skills show confidence and leadership, while weak ones show self-consciousness and ineptitude. If you speak and present well, you will be noticed and dramatically increase your chances of being offered better opportunities.

So how can you make your speech engaging? The first step is to decide on the message that you want to communicate to your audience and then decide whether or not that message is relevant to your audience. If your audience does not care about your theme, then your speech will fall on deaf ears. You are taking up people's valuable time so your message should be pertinent. In one business survey, respondents replied that 38% of presenters gave speeches that were not relevant to them.

The next thing to do is follow three simple rules; prepare, practice and practice. By practicing, you will become more confident and decrease your stage fright. Practice does not mean memorization rather making your delivery sound natural, passionate and confident. An effective suggestion for improving your speech is to rehearse in front of supportive coworkers or friends, so they can give you some feedback.

As for PowerPoint slides, keep them simple. Do not put so much information in the slides that suddenly your audience's eyes become glazed over due to information overload. Keep font size to a minimum of 30 points and have no more than six brief points or one image per slide. A slide should be a jumping off point for a speech not the core of the talk. Remember that you should spend more time practicing your speech than preparing your slides, as your delivery is more important than the slides.

There are numerous more techniques to improve public speaking, but the key is to put yourself in your audience's shoes when you give a speech. Would you enjoy listening to this speech or presentation? Would you feel engaged? Better informed? If no, then you have not followed the Golden Rule of public speaking as you have made others listen to a speech, you would not have wanted to listen to.

© David Baird

The Golden Rule

Activity Sheet

True or False Activity

According to the reading, circle whether the statements below are true or false

1. Jesus told his followers, "Do unto others as you wish to do unto them. — True/False
2. Great presentation skills can help people be promoted. — True/False
3. The quality of your product is more important than your speech. — True/False
4. Your coworkers will not look forward to watching your speeches if you are a bad speaker. — True/False
5. Your topic should be relevant to your audience. — True/False
6. A business survey showed that nearly 2/5 of speakers gave speeches on topics they had no idea about. — True/False
7. An important result of an excellent presentation could be camaraderie. — True/False
8. For speeches, people should plan, prepare and practice. — True/False
9. Each PowerPoint slide should have a lot of graphs and charts. — True/False
10. Speakers should spend more time rehearsing their speech than making slides. — True/False

Ranking My Presentation

Rate the last presentation you gave based on the survey below. Circle your ranking.
1 is perfect 10 is terrible

1. I was well rehearsed.
   1   2   3   4   5   6   7   8   9   10
2. I knew my topic.
   1   2   3   4   5   6   7   8   9   10
3. My introduction grabbed the audience.
   1   2   3   4   5   6   7   8   9   10
4. I looked at the audience over 90% of the time.
   1   2   3   4   5   6   7   8   9   10
5. I looked and sounded comfortable and confident when I was speaking.
   1   2   3   4   5   6   7   8   9   10
6. I moved around and used expressive body language.
   1   2   3   4   5   6   7   8   9   10
7. My PowerPoint slides were simple and easy to understand.
   1   2   3   4   5   6   7   8   9   10
8. The benefits I spoke about matched my audience's wants and needs.
   1   2   3   4   5   6   7   8   9   10
9. My message was clear and focused and I spoke within the allotted time.
   1   2   3   4   5   6   7   8   9   10
10. I ended with a strong conclusion.
    1   2   3   4   5   6   7   8   9   10

Classroom Discussion Questions

Please discuss the questions below with your classmates. Ask follow up questions if needed and give detailed answers.

1. Do you follow the Golden Rule?
2. Do you follow the Golden Rule about public speaking?
3. What is the best speech you have ever heard?
4. What is the worst speech you have ever heard?
5. Why do people usually deliver poor speeches?
6. Are public speaking skills something innate or something learnt?
7. After reading this article, how will you change your approach to public speaking?
8. What additional tips would you offer for a business presentation?

Write additional discussion questions for class discussions based on the topic in the article.

a) _____
b) _____
c) _____
d) _____

The Golden Rule

Lesson Notes

_____
_____
_____
_____
_____
_____
_____
_____
_____
_____

Today's Vocabulary

Words	Synonym	Antonym	Definition

Collocations/Phrases	Definition

What did I learn today?
_____
_____
_____
_____

What do I need to improve?
_____
_____
_____
_____

My homework for next class
_____
_____
_____

Eureka!

Warm Up

Creative Challenge Activity
Before reading the article, choose whether the following statements below are true or false

1. The more varied the people someone interacts with, the more creative the person is. — True/False
2. The development of cities has accelerated humanity's progress. — True/False
3. Big monetary incentives increase motivation, which then increases innovation productivity. — True/False
4. Not being susceptible to distraction can be beneficial in the creative process. — True/False
5. Being either tired or having a drink can sometimes help people be creative. — True/False
6. Under a lot of stress is the ideal state to create in. — True/False
7. Very knowledgeable experts can only solve hard problems. — True/False
8. Creativity has seldom been studied by academics. — True/False
9. Very few people have the talent to be creative. — True/False

Good or Bad Advice to Enhance Creativity
Read the suggestions below and decide if you think these are good or bad suggestions to enhance creativity. Discuss your answers and reasons with your classmates.

a) Brainstorm ideas on one topic onto a large piece of paper. Do not edit the ideas, just write them down.
b) Go for a walk so you can allow yourself to play with an idea.
c) Put your theory down on paper.
d) Ask the same question at least twenty times and give a different answer each time.
e) Follow what the experts say and do not mention your observations to them.
f) Combine some of the features of two different objects or ideas to see if you can create several more.
g) Keep to the same routine every day. For example, walk the same route to work or school every day.
h) Let your mind be influenced by new stimuli such as music you do not usually listen to.
i) Be open to ideas when they are still new.
j) Do not ask any questions because they might make you look stupid.

Fill in the Blank Activity
Put the right form of "create" in the sentences below.

create   created   creative   creation   creativity

1. I am trying to _____ a masterpiece.
2. This is going to take some highly _____ thinking.
3. _____ does not come cheap.
4. We need to _____ order out of chaos.
5. Your manager's rigid approach to everything stifles _____.
6. The _____ of the universe and man described in the Bible is believed by many conservative Christians.
7. Our company needs to encourage more _____ in all divisions.
8. I am just not in a _____ mood today.
9. Norika _____ a scene in the restaurant when I broke up with her.
10. When and how the universe was _____ is one of the big questions in physics.

Vocabulary Activity
Put in either *discover*, *invent* or *create* in the sentences below in the proper forms

1. Johann Galle _____ Neptune based upon the calculations of John Adams and Urbain LeVierrer
2. No one knows who _____ the wheel.
3. Shakespeare _____ some of the most beautiful lines in the English language.
4. Isaac Newton _____ the law of universal gravitation.
5. Archimedes _____ the Archimedes screw which is used for irrigation.
6. Lego lets children _____ all sorts of interesting things.

Eureka!

According to legend, 2,300 years ago, Greek mathematician Archimedes stepped into his bathtub and noticed that the water level rose, which caused him to experience an epiphany that the volume of water displaced must be equal to the volume of his submerged body. He responded by yelling "Eureka!" and running naked through the streets. Archimedes had solved the mystery of how to measure precisely the volume of an irregular object.

This myth illustrates that people often come up with their best insights when not at their desks, but engaged in other activities. The when, the where and the how people are creative is being studied by psychologists, neurologists, geneticists and even architects. Presently they do not have all the answers, but have produced some fresh and interesting insights.

One interesting finding shows that creative people need to communicate with other people. This finding goes against the stereotype of the lone inventor working in isolation and achieving some historic breakthrough. The truth is most of the greatest discoveries are often made when people and ideas interact with each other. Because of this finding, architects and designers are now devising workplaces and office complexes that foster interaction and collaboration between different departments.

The story of Archimedes and his eureka moment, it highlights two important components connected to the creative process, the epiphany and associative thinking. An epiphany is a sudden enlightening realization that lets a problem be seen from a fresher and different perspective. Many scientists tell compelling stories of when exactly they made their amazing discovery yet the reality is different. Upon examination of their work notes, it shows that they often had a series of small epiphanies and not just one big one. The creative person will work on a problem for days, weeks or even years

Associative thinking or free association is when the mind wanders onto other topics and outside their field to find new methods, concepts, and ideas to apply and utilize them to solve a problem. When people are away from work, their minds relax and they start to freely associate ideas and information more randomly.

An example of interaction, associative thinking and the need for time is Charles Darwin and his development of the Theory of Evolution. The first germ of an idea about evolution originated at the end of the HMS Beagle voyage in 1836. In the next twenty years besides spending time on the theory's development, Darwin wrote on geology and South America, and read and discussed with the leading scientists in the UK, Europe and the USA on new scientific theories and discoveries. To recap, Darwin worked on the problem for over a long time span, interacted with people to discuss evolution, looked at concepts and theories outside his field, and applied them. Finally, in 1859, he published *On the Origin of Species*.

If an organization needs an example from business, it can look at two very innovative companies, 3M and Google. 3M provides a diverse number of centers and organizes forums and events so the various research and product divisions can pool ideas. Results of that collaboration have been applying dental technology to car parts and using a low tack adhesive to paper to create Post it Notes. Google is famous for allowing many of its employees to spend 20% of their work time on a project of their choosing. It has led to the development of Google News, Gmail and most importantly for Google, AdSense, which accounts for 25% of its revenues

Management's challenge is to create an atmosphere and structure to enable their people to think and do things differently so creativity can thrive. They have to realize that patience, a certain amount of freedom and socialization is beneficial for the company. Creativity and innovation are indispensable for any organization to survive in the long run.

© David Baird

Eureka!

Activity Sheet

True or False Quiz

According to the reading, circle whether the statements below are true or false

1. Around 2,300 years ago, Greek mathematician Archimedes slipped in his bathtub. — True/False
2. Yelling "Eureka!" is an expression used when obtaining a sudden insight. — True/False
3. Psychologists, neurologists and geneticists are trying to find when and where people are creative — True/False
4. The lone inventor story of working in isolation and achieving some historic breakthrough is quite common. — True/False
5. An epiphany is a sudden understanding, which allows a problem to be, approached from a similar perspective. — True/False
6. A wandering mind can be helpful during the creative process. — True/False
7. Charles Darwin quickly came up with the Theory of Evolution. — True/False
8. Generally, creative people enjoy working in isolation. — True/False
9. Google and 3M are unique companies that other companies should not imitate. — True/False

Vocabulary Activity

A. Match the words from the reading on the left with similar meaning words on the right

1. epiphany
2. precisely
3. stereotypical
4. components
5. isolation
6. enlightening
7. randomly
8. collaboration
9. indispensable

a) informative
b) factors
c) obligatory
d) realization
e) aimlessly
f) conventional
g) accurately
h) partnership
i) seclusion

B Now choose five of the words from the above vocabulary exercise and write five sentences below using each of those words in a sentence.
Example: *I experienced an **epiphany** in my shower this morning.*

a) _____
b) _____
c) _____
d) _____
e) _____

Classroom Discussion Questions

Write discussion questions for class discussions based on the topic in the article. Try to use the idioms from this article in your questions.

a) _____
b) _____
c) _____
d) _____
e) _____

Additional Questions for Discussion

Discuss the questions below with your classmates and make sure they give reasons.

1. Have you ever experienced an epiphany? What was it?
2. How would you define creativity?
3. Do you think scientists have to be creative?
4. Where and when do you come up with your best ideas?
5. How would you foster creativity in your organization?
6. Which company do you think is innovative or creative?

Eureka

Lesson Notes

_____
_____
_____
_____
_____
_____
_____
_____
_____
_____

Today's Vocabulary

Words	Synonym	Antonym	Definition

Collocations/Phrases	Definition

What did I learn today?
_____
_____
_____
_____

What do I need to improve?
_____
_____
_____
_____

My homework for next class
_____
_____
_____

Play Ball!

Warm Up

Baseball Idioms Activities

A. Read the sentences below then try to match the meanings of the idioms with their definitions.
   a) I can't even **reach first base** with my boss on how to change our team's goals.
   b) I did not expect his response. He really **threw** me **a curve**.
   c) Everything has changed so it's a **whole new ballgame**.
   d) Either **play ball** with us or leave.
   e) I'm just going to call and **touch base** with my wife.

   1. reach first base   a) to cooperate with someone
   2. throw (someone) a curve   b) a new set of circumstances
   3. whole new ballgame   c) to make a small step forward in a project
   4. play ball   d) to briefly talk with someone
   5. touch base   e) to surprise someone by doing something unexpected

B. Read the sentences below then try to match the meanings of the idioms with their definitions.
   a) This morning, **right off the bat** I had to settle an argument between two team members.
   b) I don't like negotiating with that guy as he always **plays hardball**.
   c) We need to call in our **ace** if we want this to succeed.
   d) Many appearances with **heavy hitters** from the party helped him win the election.
   e) Give me a persuasive argument supported with solid data and I'll **go to bat for** you.

   1. right off the bat   a) to be or act tough, aggressive
   2. play hardball   b) elite performer
   3. ace   c) at the start
   4. go to bat for someone   d) a powerful or commanding person
   5. heavy hitter   e) to help or support someone

C. Fill in the gaps in the conversation below with the 10 baseball expressions from the previous exercises.

   A: Hi Grace. How can I help you today?
   B: Well Stuart I just wanted to _____ with you about our meeting yesterday with the Stengel negotiations.
   A: How did it go?
   B: _____ I could tell they were going to _____ I was expecting a friendly meeting where we would both discuss our needs and goals and create a win-win situation. Instead, they brought in Michael Kuzak from *McKenzie and Brackman*.
   A: Who's Michael Kuzak?
   B: He's a high priced lawyer, known as a(n) _____ negotiator a real _____.
   A: So they _____ you _____ So what did you do?
   B: I just listened to their demands and realized we were not going to even _____ I mean, it's now a _____.
   A: What do you want to do now?
   B: I don't know as their change in strategy has made me think that I don't even think we should _____ with them.
   A: Are you saying you want to break off negotiations?
   B: Yes. When we spoke to them, we told them we were looking for a mutually beneficial association. It was all supposed to be cooperative and friendly. They just do not realize that they are not our only option.
   A: Listen don't worry, I'll _____ if anyone complains. I trust you'll do the right thing.

Play Ball!

For many people, business is all about winning and losing. Therefore, it is not uncommon to hear some businessperson use a variety of sports idioms as sport like business is an activity where competition is an essential element.

In many countries, sports and sporting events are the national pastime, so sports idioms have infiltrated everyday usage. Learning sports idioms does not mean becoming a sports fanatic, but attaining a basic understanding of some of the more popular sports would not hurt. Understanding the game would give some context to the idioms making them easier to understand.

In American English, the most popular sources of idioms are baseball, American football, golf, horseracing and boxing. Of all the sports, baseball, which is described as America's national pastime, has contributed a considerable number of idioms to American English. French historian, Jacques Barzun once said, "Whoever wants to know the heart and mind of America had better learn baseball." He could also have been referring to American English.

One reason why baseball idioms are so popular has to do with the history of sport in America. Baseball has existed for over 150 years and its two major professional leagues are each over 110 years old. The professional leagues for the other popular major (basketball, hockey and American football) were established later, and did not become popular until after WWII.

Additionally how fans followed baseball helped increase its impact on the language. Since the 1920s, people have been listening to baseball games on the radio. As baseball is a rather slow-paced game with considerable stoppage in play, the announcers had to fill in the time with chatter. On top of that, a major league baseball team played over 140 games each year and every one of them was broadcasted over the radio. This huge amount of time lead to baseball idioms and phrases being widely understood and adopted into everyday language.

Moreover, people did not just hear numerous baseball games, but they also read about it. As baseball was widely followed, the newspapers spent a significant part of their sports coverage on baseball. People would read everyday about their heroes and teams in some very entertaining prose. Additionally some great American writers such as Mark Twain, Ernest Hemingway, John Steinbeck and John Updike have used baseball in their novels.

It is no wonder that baseball expressions have become an integral part of American English. It is not just baseball fans who use the language but Americans from all walks of life. President Obama stated in a news conference, "You hit singles, you hit doubles; every once in a while we may be able to hit a home run." He was describing the different degrees of success. In job ads, a popular line is that working at this company is an opportunity "to join the big leagues" (Someone can join an elite company).

Idioms are a difficult thing to understand like some of baseball's rules. However learning idioms is important, as they are natural to native speakers and are often used. So *step up to the plate and don't be afraid to swing away*. (Put yourself in a position to try)

Play Ball!
Activity Sheet

Reading Comprehension Activity

According to the reading, circle whether the statements below are true or false

1. Businesspeople often use expression from sports. — True/False
2. The most popular sources of American sport idioms are baseball, soccer and golf. — True/False
3. Professional leagues for other popular major sports are basketball, hockey and American football. — True/False
4. French historians are big fans of baseball. — True/False
5. Since the 1920s, people have been watching baseball games on TV. — True/False
6. Some famous modern American writers have referred to baseball in their novels. — True/False
7. Even Barack Obama uses sport idioms when he speaks. — True/False
8. Some employees describe working at their company as being in the major leagues. — True/False
9. Idioms are hard for non-native sport fans to understand and master. — True/False

Vocabulary Activity

A. Match the words from the reading on the left with similar meaning words on the right

1. element
2. infiltrated
3. pastime
4. impact
5. stoppage
6. chatter
7. coverage
8. prose
9. step up to the plate
10. swing away

a) entered
b) to prepare to do a task
c) influence
d) component
e) entertainment
f) talk
g) text
h) try
i) halting
j) reporting

B. Now, choose five of the words from the above vocabulary exercise and write five sentences below using each of those words in a sentence.
Example: My favorite *pastime* is studying English.

a) _____
b) _____
c) _____
d) _____
e) _____

Classroom Discussions Questions

Write discussion questions for class discussions based on the topic in the article. Next, ask your classmates your questions and make sure they give reasons.

a) _____
b) _____
c) _____
d) _____

Additional Questions for Discussion

Please discuss the questions below with your classmates. Ask your classmates follow up questions if needed. In addition, give detailed reasons to your answers.

1. What is your favorite sport? Are you an avid fan?
2. Are you good at any sports? If yes, which ones?
3. What do you think is the most popular sport in the world?
4. Do you think playing team sports when younger prepares people to be better team players when they are adults?
5. Do you try to hit home runs or are you a singles hitter?
6. When do you play hardball?
7. What do you do when someone throws you a curve?

Play Ball!
Lesson Notes

_____

Today's Vocabulary

Words	Synonym	Antonym	Definition

Collocations/Phrases	Definition

What did I learn today?
_____

What do I need to improve?
_____

My homework for next class
_____

© David Baird

Miscellaneous Articles Vocabulary Review

Wonder Word Activity

Step One
Answer all of the clues for the words in the columns below. Many words are from the previous units. The words are also in the box of letters below

1. Sudden insight
   _ e _ p _ _ _ _ a _ y
2. Exactly *Precisely*
3. Make Clear
   e _ _ l _ _ _ _ _ n
4. "Please _ p _ _ up and let me in."
5. Required
   _ _ e d _ _
6. Secured
   g _ u _ _ _ _ _ _ _
7. Bet _ _ a _ g _ _
8. Economic alliance
   _ a _ t _ l
9. "A Day in the _ i _ f _ e" Beatles song
10. "The angry customer _y _ l l _ _ at me."
11. Strategy _ _ a _
12. List ending abbr. _ _ c
13. Team c _ _ t _ _ n
14. Ingredient
    _ l e _ _ _ _ t
15. "P _ _ d _ and Joy" Motown song
16. Long story _ e _ _ c Kingdom _ m _ _ r _
17. Sway
    i _ n _ _ _ _ n _
18. What an accounting firm did. _ u d _ _ _ _ d
19. "It's _ u r _ -fire, won't fail."
20. Talk _ h _ a _ _ _ _ r
21. "Baseball, America's p _ _ _ _ m _ "
22. Text _ r _ _ s _
23. Widespread
    _p _ _ _ a _ _ t
24. Parts
    c _ _ _ _ _ _ e _ t s
25. Deceive _ _ _ _ _ c _k
26. Energetic _ i v _ _ _ _
27. "The Earth is not f _ _ _ _ "
28. _ r _ c _ _ _ go up when there is high demand.
29. A very long time _ _ o _
30. Referred to _ _ t _ d
31. Golf goal _ _ _
32. "Life is a _ a _ l _ told by an idiot."
33. Small island _ _ _ l e
34. Paid Athlete _ _ _ o
35. "P _ _ n _ Man" Billy Joel song
36. Keyed in
    _ _ _ p _ t _ t _ d
37. Overflow _ l o _ _ _
38. Connection
    _c _ r _ r _ _ _ _ _ n
39. Chiefly
    _ r _ m _ _ _ _ l _
40. "It's _ _ n _ _ Rock and Roll" Rolling Stones Song
41. "_ _ v _ Jeans" Brand name
42. A musical drama
    _ p _ r _
43. Mistake _ a _ u _ _ _
44. A high price
    _ o _ _ _ _ l l a _
45. Diplomacy _ _ c t _

Step Two
All the words in the columns above appear in the box below. When you find a word, circle it. The words can be vertical, horizontal or diagonal. Some of the diagonal words right to left. There will be eleven letters remaining. Unscramble those letters to spell the wonder word phrase.

E	P	I	C	E	L	E	M	E	N	T	P	P
M	P	R	O	S	E	S	U	R	E	R	R	A
P	R	I	M	A	R	I	L	Y	E	I	E	S
I	E	H	P	R	O	I	I	I	D	C	V	T
R	C	O	O	H	F	P	V	E	E	K	A	I
E	I	E	N	E	A	E	E	H	D	C	L	M
I	S	L	E	T	L	N	L	N	T	I	E	E
N	E	F	N	O	N	L	Y	E	I	I	N	A
F	L	A	T	P	R	I	C	E	S	E	T	U
L	Y	U	S	D	C	G	U	A	R	D	E	D
U	F	L	O	O	D	H	C	W	V	T	T	I
E	P	T	A	L	E	T	A	A	A	Y	E	T
N	I	Y	E	L	L	E	D	T	R	G	R	E
C	A	P	T	A	I	N	P	U	T	T	E	D
E	N	A	A	R	O	P	E	R	A	E	E	R
C	O	R	R	E	L	A	T	I	O	N	R	L

Wonder Word Phrase (hint sports idiom) _ _ _ _ _ _   _ _ _ _ _ _ _

Miscellaneous Articles Vocabulary Review

Sentence Scramble

Unscramble the words below and put them into the proper order to create sentences.

1. He/unprepared/inept/but/an/is/not/employee/ace

2. with/advice/sage/curve/thrown/a/helped/was/me/when/She/I

3. that/I/His/shocked/isolated/revelation/felt/me/and

4. His/encouraging/anecdotes/built/and/the/team/feeling/comments/of/ camaraderie

5. playing/hitter/are/so/need/They/we/a/heavy/obviously/hardball

6. Right/he/off/told/the/me/he/had/bat/was/craving/pizza

7. a/more/an/epiphany/night/that/Last/nuanced/I/had/we/a/need/strategy

8. His/about/the/on/ears/the/IT/deaf/department/complaints/fell

9. that/realistic/or/Yuka/are/not/objections/usually/raises/pertinent

10. tried/wear/with/down/They/tedious/to/until/we/us/discussions/agreed

Public Speaking

The teacher will choose one of the following topics and you will have 10 seconds to prepare a short speech on that topic. Your teacher will decide how long the speech will be.

Stereotypes	The Golden Rule	Feedback
Epiphany	Public Speaking	Gambling
Baseball	Creativity	Strategy
Negotiating	Collaboration	Success
Poker	Competition	Good Looks
Wisdom	Bureaucracy	Hard work
Listening	Professionalism	Preparation
Coffee	Rejection	First Impressions
The Internet	Vacations	Ageism
Dress Codes	Style	Groupthink
Accountability	Triumph	Disaster

Textbook Review

Comprehension Review

Answer the following questions based on the articles in the textbook.

1. According to the textbook, what sport has generated many idioms?
2. Which character from Shakespeare is mentioned in an article?
3. What is often offered at a business meeting in America?
4. What does adage mean?
5. Name three writers mentioned in the textbook
6. What does epiphany mean?
7. What is the Golden Rule?
8. Why is 1984 important?
9. Why was Google's Parisian Love advertisement significant?
10. In how many foreign languages can you write hello?
11. In how many foreign languages can you write no?
12. Who is Edward T. Hall?
13. How does height help people be successful?
14. Do acquisitions usually succeed or fail?
15. What is EQ?
16. What does low context culture mean?
17. What is a devil's advocate?
18. What does red tape mean?
19. What year did the dot com bubble reach its peak?
20. What is the most socially condoned form of prejudice?

Discussion Questions

Please discuss the questions below with your classmates. Ask your classmates follow up questions if needed. In addition, give detailed reasons to your answers.

1. Can you name an innovative or creative company?
2. Which company do you think would be good to work for?
3. What advice would you give people worried about privacy?
4. Are the majority of your decisions based on logic or emotion?
5. Do you dress for style or for comfort?
6. What do you do when someone throws you a curve?
7. Are people becoming less sociable because of computers and the Internet?

Additional Questions for Discussion

Write additional questions for class discussion based on the topics discussed in the textbook.

a) _____
b) _____
c) _____

Photo Credits

The cover was designed by Lapis Design who I have to thank for their advice and support. The main sources of the photos and images are from FreeImages.com, iStockPhoto.com, FreeDigitalPhotos.net and Wikipedia.

P 6 Figure and translate button comes from freedigitalphotos.net
P 8 Girl having sushi by TrentVino from iStockphoto
P 12 Ishin Denshin Kanji by Masami Kojima, copyright is owned by the author
P 16 Coffee and Doughnut Photo by Stuart Miles and the bottom corner photo is from phasinphoto with both from FreeDigitalPhotos.net.
P 20 The "No" Image was created by the author.
P 24 Image by *jscreations* from FreeDigitalPhotos.net
P28 Photos of Peter Drucker and W. Edwards Deming from Wikipedia Game Player by mzacha from freeimages.com
P 32 Figures in a circle is from freeimages.com
P34 Rat by puellakas from and snake by creator100 from freeimages.com and snake
P 38 People with bat and knife by Skip O'Donnell from iStcockphoto
P 42 Othello and Iago image is public domain image from Charles and Mary Lamb, Tales from Shakespeare, downloaded from Wikipedia
46 I'm Shy Photo by Imagery Majestic from freedigitalphotos.net
P49 Photos of Ken Watanabe, Dalai Lama, Masayoshi Son and Johnny Depp are from Wikipedia
Photo of Yuki Amami is from Daily Celebrity
P 50 Image by Spekulator from freeimages.com
P54 Man in suit by imagerymajestic and man in shorts and t-shirt by stockimages from freedigitalphotos.com
P 62 Naked legs by Spanishalex from iStockphoto.com
P 66 Staff walking photo is by YinYang from iStockphoto.com
P 70 Sleeping man is by Tagstock1 from istockphoto and chairs at beach shore is by arinas74 from freeimages.com.
P 74 People attending a training session is by shironosov from iStockiphoto
P 78 Older woman comes from gronvik from free images .com. Happy American Businessman by Patrisyu courtesy of free digital photos.com. Young oriental woman is by stock images courtesy of freedigital photos.com. Middle Aged man is by stock images courtesy of freedigital photos.com. Older man by Ambro courtesy of freedigital photos.com. Middle Aged man is by stock images, courtesy of freedigital photos.com. Young businessperson is by David Castillo Dominici, courtesy of freedigitalphotos.com Young businessperson is by tozz courtesy of freedigitalphotos.com.
P82 Eye tear stockimage is by idea go courtesy of freedigitalphotos.com
P 84 Coin is by yochim from freeimages.com
P 88 Geek is by sdricPhoto, from iStock photo.com and the man in the suit is by imagery majestic, courtesy of freedigitalphotos.com
P 91 Eye tear stock image is by idea go courtesy of freedigitalphotos.com
P 92. Cameras and hacking image are by Victor Habbick courtesy of freedigitalphotos.com. The Facebook, Foursquare and Twitter logos are property of those companies and are their trademarks. The use of the trademarks is under fair use and solely for the purposes of description and identification.
P 96 The data image is by flaivoloka courtesy of freeimages.com
P100 Figure on Success Button is by Stuart Miles courtesy of FreeDigitalphotos.com
P 102 The man sitting comes courtesy of freedigitalphotos.net
P 106 .The violinist is by Kontrec, courtesy of iStockphotos.com and the work illustration is by Stuart Miles courtesy of freeddigitalphotios.net
P 110 The Beatles photo comes from iStockphoto.com
P 114 Luck photo is by Stuart Miles from FreeDigitalphotos.com
P 116 Tall man and figurine is by Marcus74id at free digital photos
P 120 Signpost is by cobrasoft courtesy of freeimages.com
P 126 Business figures image is by cooldesign courtesy of free digital photos
P 128 Dollar funnel is by Leonardini courtesy of freeimages.com
P 132 top Right photo is by ayzek, courtesy of istockphotos.com and Risk images created by jscreations courtesy of freedigitalphotos.com
P 136 Original image of scales is by darktaco courtesy of freeimages.com
P 140 *The Buck No Longer Stops Here* photo comes from Wikipedia
P 144 The marketing image is by Stuart Miles courtesy of Freedigitalphotos. Eye chart is from ponsulak by freedigitalphotos.com
P 146 Facebook, Instagram, Pinterest and Twitter logos are property of those companies and are their trademarks. The use of the trademarks is used under fair use and solely for the purposes of description and identification. All photos from Wikipedia.
P 150 The Eiffel tower photo is by 01099 courtesy of freeimages.com The Google screenshot is used under fair use and solely for the purposes of description and identification. The trademark and logo are the property of Google.
P 154 The Coca Cola bottle photo is from sasicd from Free Images.com. The picture of the Ginza Gap store is from iStockphoto.com.
P 157 Japanese businesswoman is from iStockphoto.com
P 164 The ear is from a personal photo and copyright is owned by the author.
P 168 Poker chips photo is by vierdie.nl courtesy of freeimages.com
P 172 Jesus on the Mount by Carl Heinrich Bloch is a public domain image and came from Wikipedia. The sleeping people photo is by vitranc from iStockiphoto.
P 176 Archimedes painting is by Fetti and comes courtesy of Wikipedia. The Darwin photo is from istockphotos.com
P 180 The baseball image is by ba1969 from freeimages.com

All rights reserved; no part of this publication may be reproduced, stored in a retrieval system, or transmitted in any form or by any means electronic, mechanical, photocopying, recording or otherwise without the prior written permission of David Baird.

Please visit our website at pigrouppublishing.com

© David Baird

Story Ideas and Credits

Many of the opinions and ideas originated from other sources and I often filtered them to write the articles. Below is a brief bibliography and I have to say unfortunately it is not complete. The majority of these articles were not originally intended to be a book but were mainly used for one class that I taught. For any source not properly cited, I offer my apologies. General references are Merriam-Webster Dictionary, Oxford Collocation Dictionary Thesauraus.com, Wikipedia and Investopedia.

1. **You Use Chopsticks Well** was born out of hearing that line many times in Japan and thinking that even the most innocuous comments can be taken the wrong way. Also I would never tell a foreigner that they use a knife and fork well.
2. **Ishin Denshin** terms come from *The Japanese Have a Word for It by* Boye Lafayette De Mente.
3. **Coffee and Doughnuts** came from my attending meetings in Canada and comparing it to meetings in Japan.
4. **No is not a Four Letter Word** was hearing students and Japanese acquaintances often saying *maybe* but meaning no.
5. **Ambiguity, Vagueness and the Unknown** is mainly based on *Hidden Differences* by Edward T. Hall.
6. **Looking in the Mirror** sources are Wikipedia, YouTube, and druckerinstitute.com

Some of the questions in the discussion in the cross culture review came from Christine Bauer-Ramazani of St. Michael's College, Vermont.

7. **Another Day in the Rat Race** idea originally came from an old lesson from a GEOS textbook Prep E.
8. The author of the assertiveness survey in the **Fourth Type**, I could not find. It appears on many different websites and in books with no authorship cited. The advice tips mainly come from WikiHow but many other sites have similar advice tips.
9. **I Wear My Hear upon My Sleeve's** idea came from a friend who often used the used that line and my thinking on who said it. The hidden agenda and the people comes from my experience in politics many years ago.
10. The idea from **I'm Shy** came from year's of experience and reading
11. The main sources for **Being Great** come from two of Jim Collins books' *Good to Great* and *How the Mighty Fall*.
12. **Clothes Make the Man and Woman** originated from the quote by Linda Ellerbee and changes I have seen in the last few years in Japan.
13. The original idea on **My Boss has No Clothes** came from an article about young employees disagreeing with their boss. I cannot find the original source but there are countless articles on this subject.
14. **It's Just Business, Nothing Personal** came from my research on teaching a course for Japanese managers on how to evaluate foreign staff.
15. **I'm so Tired; My Mind is on the Blink** is a reaction from teaching Japanese for the last 14 years and their undervaluing the importance of rest and vacation.
16. **LIFO** is my observation of some organizations not understanding how language training works. The survey comes from the website https://www.surveyshare.com
17. The idea of **Help Wanted, Help Wanted, But only If** came from my experience and my girlfriend's experience age discrimination as well as sudden glut of articles in 2014 about age discrimination in Silicon Valley.
18. **Two Sides of the Coin** was sparked by my negative reaction to technology evangelists. Also I came across a few articles that showed that using books is more effective that using the computer for studying and retention.
19. The background for **Geeks vs. Suits** came first from *Triumph of the Nerds*, an old PBS documentary and then a host of articles on friction in IT companies.
20. **1984 May Still Be Coming** comes from my own fears. This article was written well before Eric Snowden's revelation about the NSA.
21. **Noise from the Knowledge** originated from Nathan Silver's book *The Signal and the Noise* and was also influenced by Nassim Nicholas Taleb *Fooled by Randomness*

The overall idea for the Success articles came from Outliers by Malcolm Gladwell.

22. The background for Success is **Not in Our Stars (Part 1)** came from both *Outliers* and Daniel Goleman's *Emotional Intelligence*.
23. The first draft of **Success is Not in Our Stars (Part 2)** came from Outliers but then I came across Geoff Colvin's *Talent is Overrated* and then revised this unit. If success is important to you, I recommend both these books.
24. **Success Is Not In Our Stars (Part 3)** was the last article I wrote and the idea came from a speech by Angela Duckworth I saw via the TED website. I also suggest checking the Stanford Marshmallow experiments by Walter Mischel.
25. The idea of **Success Is Not In Our Stars (Part 4)** comes from Malcolm Gladwell's *Outliers*.
26. The idea of **Success Is Not In Our Stars (Part 5)** comes not from Malcolm Gladwell's *Outliers* but another of his book's *Blink*. Although the importance of looks and height has been reported on in the last 25 years.
27. **Meeting Triumph and Disaster** was inspired by the financial crisis and the rise of CEO salaries. The Rudyard Kipling quote I had never heard before but after using it, I started seeing it quoted in articles and movies.
28. The idea of **Organic vs. Non-Organic** first came from reading an article in *Intelligent Business*.
29. **The Importance of Questions** also originated from my observations of the 2008 financial crisis.
30. The background for **A Delicate Balance** came from Jim Collin's two books *How the Mighty Fall* and *Good to Great* plus a few other articles by Jim Collins that I found on the Internet.
31. **The Buck No Longer Stops Anywhere** comes from watching corporate scandals over the last 30 years and seeing how companies react to them. The end part stating what type of problems came from an HBR article by Brian Barnier.
32. **Walk a Mile in My Shoes** comes from my own studies at university. The 4Cs was taught after I left university. The two main developers of the concept are Robert F. Lauterborn and Koichi Shimizu.
33. The background for **Weapons of Mass Persuasion** is just putting many topics together.
34. The idea of **Parisian Love** first came from seeing Google's Pakistani/India commercial on YouTube. It may me wonder why would an Internet company would advertise. The phrase *vaunted search engine is an indispensable enabler of modern life* comes from an article on Huffington Post by Eddie Reeves from the Reeves Strategy Group.
35. The **Eternal Marketing Buzzword, Brand** originates from my belief that brand is an overused word in marketing and many marketers do not understand all the implications of brand.
36. I was introduced to the idea from **The Disease of Not Listening** from an old lesson from a text by Geos in my formative teaching career. Since then I have seen this concept promote in articles and on websites. It is not new as it is a significant part of Dale Carnegie's *How to Win Friends and Influence People*.
37. **Play the Man Across From You** is my observation on how poker idioms are often used in business especially in negotiations.
38. **The Golden Rule** was a composite of years observing and studying public speaking.
39. The idea behind **Eureka!** was from my own curiosity on what makes people creative. After doing some reading, the book, which best explains it is Steven Johnson's *Where Good Ideas Come From*.
40. **Play Ball!** came originally from a Geos textbook and Ken Burns Baseball. While there are many sports idioms, I believe of any sport, baseball has contributed the most to American English.

Please visit our website at pigrouppublishing.com
This page has been intentionally left blank.
Please feel free to doodle on this page
Draw something great.

© David Baird

Filename:	Book Draft10.18
Directory:	E:\April 20\Articles\Articles for canada
Template:	C:\Users\David\AppData\Roaming\Microsoft\Templates\Normal.dot
Title:	1984 May Still Be Coming
Subject:	
Author:	David Baird
Keywords:	
Comments:	
Creation Date:	10/18/2015 10:36:00 PM
Change Number:	2
Last Saved On:	10/18/2015 10:36:00 PM
Last Saved By:	David
Total Editing Time:	4 Minutes
Last Printed On:	10/18/2015 10:58:00 PM

As of Last Complete Printing
- Number of Pages: 200
- Number of Words: 80,976 (approx.)
- Number of Characters: 461,564 (approx.)

www.ingramcontent.com/pod-product-compliance
Lightning Source LLC
Chambersburg PA
CBHW042301010526
44113CB00047B/2768